Ruby Violet's

ICE CREAM DREAMS

{ ICE CREAM, SORBETS, BOMBES, AND MORE }

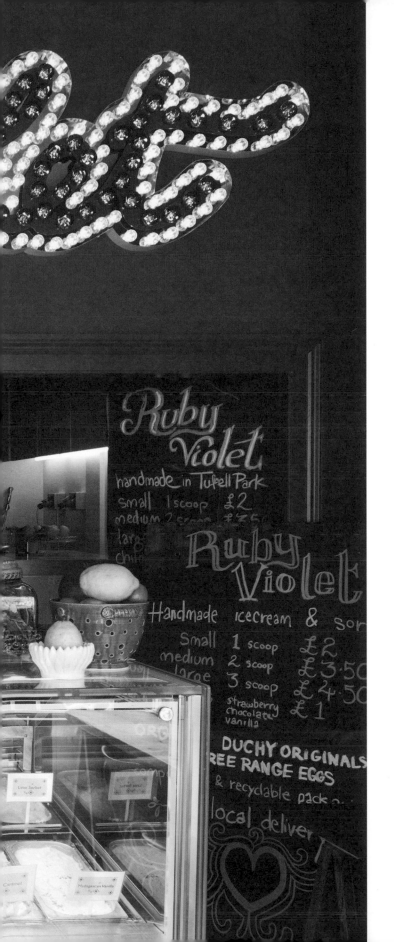

Ruby Violet's
ICE CREAM DREAMS

{ ICE CREAM, SORBETS, BOMBES, AND MORE }

FOR KIRAN

JULIE FISHER

hardie grant books
MELBOURNE · LONDON

CONTENTS

INTRODUCTION

RUBY VIOLET

Ruby Violet, my maternal grandmother, was born on the first day of spring 1906. King Edward VII was on the throne and there was a heatwave that summer. She was a strident opinionated lady with dubious driving skills and a love of Energen rolls, Penguin biscuits, golf, bridge and ice cream.

Ruby Violet loved a choc ice and I remember as a child, the crisp cracking of the thin chocolate covering and my sister and I eating slices from a block of plain ice cream squashed between a couple of wafers. When we went to my grandma's house for our holidays, we badgered her for ice cream and she usually gave in, probably because it was a good excuse for her own indulgence.

MY ICE CREAM DREAM

For 34 years I was an Editorial and Advertising Photographer and had fun working on many cookery books with great home economists in all sorts of glamorous locations (usually within the M25). But times change and as the digital global age took over I felt the need to connect once again with people, especially my local community. I love the conversations, the random nature of observations, the exchange of ideas, the enormous diversity of people coming through the door in any one day and the amazing range of talents that all lie within a small radius of NW5.

Most people love ice cream. It reminds them of happy times, childhood memories of holidays and hot sunny summers. There is a combination of nostalgia mixed with the excitement of discovering fresh new ingredients, even if you then find they appeared in *Culpeper's Complete Herbal* in 1653. It's a happy environment; ice cream makes people smile.

I started making ice cream in a small domestic ice cream maker and I tested the recipes on my enthusiastic neighbours, who were then, and still are, very forthcoming in their views. After a few months a new market opened just down the road and I took a small market stall (tested in my neighbour Stefanie's garden), outside the Tufnell Park Tavern for four hours every Saturday. The back seats were removed from my car and every weekend a spontaneously arranged crew, coerced from the immediate vicinity, lugged the essentials of an ice cream parlour: a heavy duty freezer box, two small freezers and a display freezer, three trestle tables, a gazebo and endless strings of homemade bunting, all transported in three separate journeys to the market. There we sold ice cream in cones and tubs, whatever the weather, to an increasing band of loyal and hardy customers.

After customising the car in the service of ice cream, I then turned my attentions to the 'ice cream factory', which had hitherto been our home. Large machines and freezers gradually filled our living room, our social life fizzled out and what convivial conversation there had been was now drowned out by the sound of whirring machines. A year later we moved into premises on the borders of Tufnell Park and Kentish Town, a little jewel in the heart of Fortess Road, that has been set up and run on the principle of small is beautiful and all ingredients are sustainable, fresh and local when possible.

All the ice cream is still made in small batches, using seasonal fruit prepared daily on the premises. In summer the mint, rhubarb, apples and honey are all sourced from within a few miles and the blackberries and damsons come from my home village of Flintham in Nottinghamshire.

A POTTED HISTORY

If you were royalty you would have been enjoying ice cream for more than 300 years. In 1671, King Charles II and his closest friends indulged in dishes of ice cream and strawberries, but made sure it travelled no further than the top table. Ice cream remained the preserve of the aristocracy for as long as it required an ice house, tucked away in the corner of a rural estate, and a sizeable lake or moat from which to harvest the ice.

Developments in technology and transportation during the 19th century opened up the market for ice cream among the wealthier middle classes. Ice shipped from as far afield as Scandinavia and beyond, travelled inland by canals to cavernous subterranean ice houses, from where it was distributed to the growing ice cream industry.

By the end of the 19th century an interest in and an appetite for ice cream extended throughout society. Elaborate creations coaxed from pewter moulds adorned the tables of the rising bourgeoisie, while penny scoops of ice cream were served on the street.

At the sharp end of the ice cream world were the Italians, who brought with them a culture of ice cream making. The first ice cream stall opened up outside Charing Cross Station by the entrepreneurial Carlo Gatti. But it was the elegant charm and sound business acumen of Mrs Agnes Marshall that brought ice cream making into the British domestic realm. With her energy and pioneering spirit, so marked in the Victorian era, she patented moulds and apparatus to accompany her recipe books and cookery classes. From the 20th century onwards ice cream production became fully industrialised, driven by the rapid developments in manufacturing techniques and refrigeration.

QUALITY PRODUCE

I decided right at the beginning to only use organic milk, free-range eggs and British or Fair Trade sugar. We use no artificial additives or preservatives and all our tubs and packaging are biodegradable and compostable – we even recycle our spoons.

Another of our recycling projects has been the restoration of 'Billy the van' – a 1968 English Austin, who had spent the previous 30 years lolling around in a field. Now renovated as a fully equipped ice cream van, we are able to venture out to do our good works.

The quality of ingredients is important. In these days of industrialized farming it is always good to have a sense of where ingredients come from. The ingredients in so much of supermarket ice cream, especially soft scoop, are varied and often surprising. I never imagined that you could buy ice cream that was made from pork fat, or nowdays the more environmentally controversial palm oil, but then I was also surprised that you could buy ice cream that had no whole milk or cream content whatsoever.

At Ruby Violet we're happy to keep it local, use traditional ingredients, make it by hand and talk to our customers. I am delighted to share some of our recipes with you.

The basics

❖

ESSENTIALS

FOR SUCCESSFUL ICE CREAM AND SORBETS

TEMPERATURE

Fridge temperature should be 4°C (39°F)

Freezer temperature should be -18°C (0°F)

These temperatures are important and you shouldn't just rely on the display on the fridge or freezer. There is a whole variety of inexpensive thermometers, so it would be wise to purchase one and double-check the temperature. Remember that the temperature at the top may well be higher than the bottom, as cold air sinks.

The warm milk mix needs to be cooled as quickly as possible (within 90 minutes) down to 4°C (39°F). This can be done by placing in a water bath. Do not put hot or warm mixes into the fridge as this raises the temperature within the fridge and can be dangerous.

The idea is to freeze the prepared ice cream mix as quickly as possible to reduce the size of the ice crystals, so that your ice cream is smooth and creamy. Use the fast freeze button on your freezer if you have one.

HYGIENE

Milk, cream and eggs all contain bacteria, which can cause salmonella and listeria. So when making ice cream, it is important to heat the eggs and milk or cream to the correct temperatures – this will pasteurise the eggs and kill off any bacteria in the milk and cream. Equipment, surfaces and cloths must be kept clean and sanitised.

QUALITY

We use organic milk and free-range eggs. When possible, use the highest quality ingredients you can find: you will taste the difference.

Vanilla sugar is mentioned in this book. It is easy to make. Buy some good-quality vanilla pods (preferably Madagascan as this is the best), then split them open and bury them in a jar of caster sugar. The longer you keep it, the more intense the vanilla flavour will be. Never, ever use vanilla essence as it's synthetic and won't taste as good as vanilla extract. This really is an ingredient not to skimp on!

QUANTITIES

All the recipes in this book make around 800 ml (27 fl oz) to 1 litre (1¾ pints) of ice cream or sorbet unless stated otherwise.

Alcohol, salt and sugar all act as an antifreeze, so if you add too much your ice cream or sorbet will not freeze. Sometimes this is a small price to pay as the taste is so divine, but you do need to be aware that the quantities of these ingredients will affect the way your ice cream and sorbet may freeze.

Depending on your type of ice-cream maker (we uses Cusinart), you will need to keep an eye on the ice cream or sorbet as it is churning, as the mix may increase in volume. If this happens, remove some from the bowl and continue.

1 tablespoon = 17 ml	1 egg white = approx 30 ml
1 teaspoon = 5 ml	1 lemon = 2–3 tablespoons of lemon juice
1 egg yolk = approx 15 ml	1 Seville orange = approx 75 ml (2½ fl oz) orange juice

BASIC EQUIPMENT AND WHAT YOU NEED TO GET STARTED

Ice cream maker

Non-reactive medium size saucepan

Small saucepan

Bain-marie

Small frying pan with a lid

Metal baking tray
(20 x 30 cm x 3 cm/
8 x 12 x 1½ in)

Whisk

Wooden spoon

Set of scales

Freezer

Measuring spoons:
tablespoon/teaspoon

Measuring jug

Sugar thermometer

Mixing bowl

1 litre (1¾ pints) rectangular containers to hold the ice cream

Airtight container

Rubber spatula

Food processor

Cooling rack

Net food cover

Sieve

Freezer packs

Wooden cocktail sticks

Ziploc bags

Pestle and mortar or electric spice grinder

Small clean paintbrush

Biscuit cutters, various shapes

Two stainless-steel bowls 2 cm (¾ in) apart in size

Silicone moulds, various shapes and sizes and wooden sticks

Silicone mat

Greaseproof paper or baking parchment

Flat, wide-bottomed cake slice

Metal spatula/palette knife

Fridge/freezer thermometer

Grater

Zester

Electric or glass lemon juicer

Sharp knives of different sizes

Ice cream scoop: we use Zeroll brand (see equipment page 153)

OUR BASIC ICE CREAM MIXES

As well as using these as the bases for the recipes in this book, you can use them to add your own creative inventions!

Basic Sweetened Ice Cream Mix

500 ml (17 fl oz)
double cream

250 ml (9 fl oz)
whole milk

75 g (3 oz)
granulated (raw) sugar

45 ml (1 ½ fl oz)
egg yolk
(approximately 3
large egg yolks)

pinch of salt

Make the base mix by pouring the cream, milk and sugar into a saucepan. Bring slowly to the boil then remove from the heat and allow to cool a little for about 5 minutes.

In a bowl, whisk together the egg yolks and salt until combined well.

Slowly pour the slightly cooled milk and cream on to the egg mixture, stirring constantly. Do not use boiling milk as this can turn your egg mixture into scrambled eggs.

Pour the mixture back into the saucepan and slowly heat, stirring with a wooden spoon all the time, until it has reached 85°C (185°F) but doesn't boil.

Stir at this temperature for 4 minutes or so.

It is at this point that most of the ice cream recipes in this book start.

Remove from the heat and leave to cool down to 4°C (39°F) within 90 minutes.

You can cool down the mix by placing in a pan in a sink with cold water and ice cubes, or put the mixture in a Ziploc bag which you then place in a pan of cold water with ice cubes. Do not place the uncooled mixture in the fridge or freezer.

Once cooled, keep in the fridge until ready to use, then freeze it once you have added your chosen flavourings.

Basic Unsweetened Ice Cream Mix

500 ml (17 fl oz) double cream

250 ml (9 fl oz) whole milk

45 ml (1½ fl oz) egg yolk (approximately 3 large egg yolks)

pinch of salt

Make the base mix by pouring the cream and milk into a saucepan. Bring slowly to the boil then remove from the heat and allow to cool a little for about 5 minutes.

In a bowl, whisk together the egg yolks and salt until combined well.

Slowly pour the slightly cooled milk and cream on to the egg mixture, stirring constantly. Do not use boiling milk as this can turn your egg mixture into scrambled eggs.

Pour the mixture back into the saucepan and slowly heat, stirring with a wooden spoon all the time, until it has reached 85°C (185°F) but doesn't boil.

Stir at this temperature for 4 minutes or so.

Remove from the heat and leave to cool down to 4°C (39°F) within 90 minutes.

You can cool down the mix by placing in a pan in a sink with cold water and ice cubes, or you can put the mixture in a Ziploc bag, which you then place inside a pan of cold water with ice cubes. Do not place the uncooled mixture in the fridge or freezer.

Once cooled, keep in the fridge until ready to use, then freeze it once you have added your chosen flavourings.

Helpful Hint

If you don't have an ice-cream maker, never fear. Follow the recipe as outlined, then for the final stage pour the mix into a 1 litre (1¾ pint) plastic tub, place in the freezer, and after about 1 hour (as soon as it begins to freeze at the edges), fork through to prevent ice crystals forming. This step needs to be repeated every 30–45 minutes until the mix is completely frozen (which should take approximately 3 hours).

The faster you freeze the ice cream, the smaller the ice crystals and the smoother the ice cream will be.

OUR BASIC SORBET MIXES

Sorbets are made with either sugar syrup or glucose syrup. Here are our basic recipes.

Sugar syrup

Always use equal quantities of sugar to boiling water. For example:

300 ml (10 fl oz) boiling water and 300 g (10½ oz) granulated (raw) sugar make 500 ml (17 fl oz) of sugar syrup.

To make the syrup, pour the boiling water on to the sugar and stir until dissolved.

This will keep in the fridge for two weeks. The syrup should remain clear – do not use if it goes cloudy.

Glucose syrup

Also called dextrose syrup, glucose is not as sweet as sugar, so using a glucose syrup will improve the scoopability of the sorbet. However, it does mask the flavour of the fruit and so should be used in moderation. Please be aware that this is not the same glucose syrup that you can buy pre-made in stores and supermarkets.

150 g (5 oz) caster (superfine) sugar

25 g (1 oz) glucose powder

Put the sugar and glucose powder in a saucepan with 400 ml (13½ fl oz) water and a sugar thermometer. Stir and slowly heat up to 40°C (104°F) then continue heating to 85°C (185°F). If you heat it too quickly at the beginning then it will go lumpy and you have to sieve it. Once you get above that temperature, this doesn't happen.

Remove from the heat and allow to cool. Store in the fridge.

Ice creams

Ice cream is a delicious and adaptable dessert that is really very easy to make. Whether you are craving a simple choc ice (like my grandma), or something more elaborate, so much is possible — your kitchen can become the epicentre for iced extravaganzas.

The following recipes will start you off. Once you are familiar with the basics, experiment with flavour combinations — you will have no shortage of volunteers to test and taste!

In our kitchen we use a variety of base mixes depending on the flavour we wish to create. I prefer ice cream that is not too sweet, but it is important to know that sugar is required for 'scoopability' as well as taste; it acts as an antifreeze to prevent the mix freezing into a solid block. However, too much sugar and the ice cream will be too runny.

All the recipes in this chapter make around 800 ml (27 fl oz), unless otherwise stated.

Ice creams

BLACK SESAME ICE CREAM

I have always associated black sesame seeds with Eastern Asian cuisine, so it comes as no surprise that this ice cream is a very popular flavour in China and Japan. I love black sesame for the unusual colour it creates within the ice cream palette and it tastes great! We rippled our black sesame paste with Vanilla *(see page 36),* but it can also be served with Green Tea Ice Cream *(see page 24).*

for the ice cream

800 ml (27 fl oz)
Basic Sweetened Ice
Cream Mix *(see page 14)*

160 g (5½ oz)
black sesame paste

**for the black
sesame paste**

225 g (8 oz)
black sesame seeds

225 ml (8 fl oz)
honey

To make the ice cream, simply make one quantity of the basic sweetened mix and make up to the stage before cooling.

For the black sesame paste, heat a lidded frying pan with no oil or liquid on the hob over medium heat.

Reserve 1 tablespoon of black sesame seeds and heat the rest in a hot frying pan (with the lid on as some will pop). After 1–2 minutes, shake the pan thoroughly to agitate the seeds inside.

Return the pan to the heat for another 30–60 seconds and then shake it again. You have to be careful, as you don't want to burn the seeds. If you can smell a nutty flavour coming from the pan, the seeds are thoroughly toasted and ready to use. If not, cover the pan again and return to the heat for another 30–60 seconds, then shake and check again. Repeat until the seeds are toasted.

Remove the pan from the heat and pour the sesame seeds into a bowl. (The seeds will continue cooking if you leave them in the hot pan, even after you have removed it from the heat.)

Blend the sesame seeds in a food processor until they start to release their oil. Add the honey and continue to blend until you have a paste: it will not be completely smooth. Weigh out 160 g (5½ oz), and store the rest in an airtight container for another time.

Add the sesame paste to the hot sweetened base mix, whisk well to incorporate, then cool down the mixture and churn. Scoop the churned ice cream into a container and keep in the freezer until ready to serve.

To serve, scatter the remaining tablespoon of the sesame seeds over the ice cream.

GREEN TEA ICE CREAM

In this recipe we use *Fuji Matcha*, Japanese tea *(see suppliers page 152)*, which apprently has been described as having the ability to make one's life more full and complete. I love this ice cream for the beautiful natural colour: it lifts the spirits. Great on its own or with Chocolate *(see page 28)* or Black Sesame Ice Cream *(see page 22)*.

800 ml (27 fl oz)
Basic Sweetened Ice
Cream Mix *(see page 14)*

1 tablespoon
green tea

To make the ice cream, simply make one quantity of the basic sweetened mix and make up to the stage before cooling.

In a cup measure out the green tea powder and mix well with a tablespoon of the hot mix. Once you have a smooth paste, whisk into the hot ice cream mix. Strain through a sieve if there are any lumps.

Leave the mix to cool, then place into an ice-cream maker and churn. Scoop the churned ice cream into a container and keep in the freezer until ready to serve.

SWEET BASIL ICE CREAM

Basil has become an increasingly popular ice cream flavour at Ruby Violet's. I first heard about it from the American girl running Sid's bread stall next to us at the market.

800 ml (27 fl oz)
Basic Sweetened Ice
Cream Mix (see page 14)

40 g (1½ oz)
basil leaves, stripped
from the stalk

Make one quantity of the basic sweetened mix and make up to the stage before cooling.

Add the basil leaves to the hot mix and then leave to cool. The longer you can leave the mix the more intense the flavour, as long as it is kept in the fridge and the ingredients are fresh. We leave ours to infuse for 2 days.

Strain the mix through a sieve, pressing the leaves firmly to extract all the mix. You may need to make the quantity back up to 800 ml (27 fl oz) with pasteurised milk.

Place the mix in the ice-cream maker and churn. Scoop the churned ice cream into a container and keep in the freezer until ready to serve.

WHITE CHOCOLATE TOASTED COCONUT ICE CREAM

As a child, the only time I remember seeing coconuts was at the coconut shy – I never won one though! In contrast to its hard and woody covering, the taste of coconut ice cream is surprisingly delicate. For the white chocolate, we use an organic white chocolate with 25% cocoa solids, but if you prefer, you can follow this recipe without the chocolate to make toasted coconut ice cream instead.

for the toasted coconut

1 medium coconut

for the ice cream

800 ml (27 fl oz) Basic Sweetened Ice Cream Mix (see page 14)

135 g (4½ oz) white chocolate with at least 25% cocoa solids

Crack the coconut and remove the milk: it is not needed for the recipe, so you can drink it. Using a vegetable peeler, remove the brown skin of the coconut flesh.

Grate the white coconut flesh either by hand or in food processor. The coconut will yield approximately 225 g (8 oz) of flesh.

Heat your oven to 160°C (320°F/Gas 2). Spread the grated coconut evenly on a baking tray and toast for about 30–40 minutes until golden, stirring regularly to ensure even toasting. Make sure it is quite brown – if it is under-toasted, the flavour will be too weak.

To make the ice cream, simply make one quantity of the basic sweetened mix and make up to the stage before cooling.

Add the toasted coconut to the hot sweetened base mix, reserving 1 tablespoon to sprinkle over the finished ice cream. Leave the mix to cool; the longer you can leave it, the more intense the flavour, as long as it is kept in the fridge and the ingredients are fresh.

Strain the mix through a sieve, pressing the grated coconut firmly to extract all the mix.

Finely chop the chocolate and heat in a bain-marie until melted, then whisk either by hand or in a food processor until cold, but still fluid.

Add the cold, strained coconut mix to the cold chocolate in the food processor, then whisk until evenly mixed.

Place the mix in the ice-cream maker and churn. Scoop the churned ice cream into a container and keep in the freezer until ready to serve. When serving, scatter the reserved toasted coconut over the top to decorate.

CHOCOLATE ICE CREAM

This quote for me sums up the joy of chocolate:

"Personally, I like a chocolate-covered sky. Dark, dark chocolate. People say it suits me.
I do, however, try to enjoy every colour I see – the whole spectrum.
A billion or so flavours, none of them quite the same, and a sky to slowly suck on.
It takes the edge off the stress. It helps me relax."
from *The Book Thief* by Markus Zusak

800 ml (27 fl oz)
Basic Sweetened Ice
Cream Mix *(see page 14)*

100 g (3½ oz)
plain chocolate
(at least 60% cocoa solids)
either as callets or grated

50 g (2 oz)
cocoa powder
(unsweetened)

To make the ice cream, simply make one quantity of the basic sweetened mix and make up to the stage before cooling.

Add the chocolate and cocoa powder to the hot mix and whisk in.

Leave the mix to cool, then place into the ice-cream maker and churn. Scoop the churned ice cream into a container and keep in the freezer until ready to serve.

Variations

Chilli Chocolate Ice Cream

Make the chocolate ice cream as above then, after the chocolate and cocoa powder have been whisked into the hot mix, add half a teaspoon of chilli sauce *(see suppliers page 152)*. You don't need very much: the idea is to taste the chocolate first then get a hit of the chilli 10 seconds or so after.

Chocolate Rosemary Ice Cream

I can never resist picking rosemary and pressing it between my fingers to release the fragrance and all the memories associated with it. Aphrodite, the Goddess of Love, was often depicted with a garland of rosemary as it was a symbol of fidelity. Maybe she also knew it stimulated the circulation. Use 20 g (¾ oz) fresh rosemary leaves, stripped off the stems, then added to the hot mix and leave to infuse overnight in the fridge. Strain and churn.

Chocolate Hazelnut Crunch Ice Cream

Add 100 g (3½ oz) hazelnut paste *(see suppliers page 152)*. Once the chocolate and cocoa powder have been thoroughly mixed in, whisk in the hazelnut paste slowly until fully incorporated.

BEETROOT ICE CREAM

My grandma served beetroot drowned in vinegar and sliced with salad cream and a floppy lettuce leaf. In traditional Polish style, Felicks Kalinowski served it as Borscht with a swirl of sour cream... delicious. Beetroot is an old-fashioned vegetable and much overlooked, but in ice cream it takes on a distinctly modern feel. It is especially lovely with Horseradish Ice Cream *(below)*.

4 large beetroots

800 ml (27 fl oz) Basic Sweetened Ice Cream Mix *(see page 14)*

In a saucepan, boil the beetroot, still with the skin on, until tender, then drain. Keep the tops on the beetroot, otherwise they will bleed and lose their flavour.

When the beetroot has cooled slightly, peel, then purée the flesh in a food processor. Push through a sieve if necessary: you want a smooth purée, not pieces of frozen beetroot in your ice cream.

Measure out 400 g (14 oz) of purée to use in the ice cream, then set aside to cool completely.

Make one quantity of the basic sweetened mix and leave to cool.

Stir the beetroot purée into the cold sweetened mix and churn. Scoop the churned ice cream into a container and keep in the freezer until ready to serve.

HORSERADISH ICE CREAM

Be careful where you plant it! Our garden in Flintham was overrun with horseradish: it's untameable and strangely enough, despite the name, poisonous to horses. The normally fiery horseradish is somewhat tamed in this ice cream and produces a more mellow, rounded flavour that also goes very well with the Beetroot Ice Cream *(above)*.

40 g (1½ oz) fresh horseradish root

800 ml (27 fl oz) Basic Sweetened Ice Cream Mix *(see page 14)*

Peel the horseradish root and then grate into a bowl. Set aside.

Make one quantity of the basic sweetened mix and make up to the stage before cooling.

Stir the grated horseradish into the hot mix and then leave to cool. The longer you can leave the mix, the more intense the flavour – as long as it is kept in the fridge and the ingredients are fresh. We soak ours for 1–2 days.

Strain through a sieve before placing the mix in the ice-cream maker and churning. Scoop the churned ice cream into a container and keep in the freezer until ready to serve.

HONEY ICE CREAM WITH HONEYCOMB AND TOASTED ALMONDS

This recipe contains no eggs, so is ideal for those with an egg intolerance. The honey is supplied by our local apiarist in Tufnell Park, from the hives in his garden. I would always recommend you use local honey if you can. My friend, a local bee keeper, urges us to plant more wildflowers and it is interesting that the urban bee population produces a honey with a distinctive taste as a result of the diversity of plant life within the city.

for the ice cream

500 ml (17 fl oz) double cream

250 ml (8½ fl oz) whole milk

150 g (5 oz) local honey

40 g (1½ oz) flaked almonds

for the honeycomb

150 g (5 oz) granulated (raw) sugar

50 g (2 oz) local honey

1½ teaspoons bicarbonate of soda

Heat the cream and milk in a saucepan. Once boiling, remove from the heat and add the honey. Stir well to mix and leave to cool down to 4°C (39°F) within 90 minutes.

Meanwhile, toast the almonds in a dry frying pan over a medium heat, until lightly coloured, but not burnt.

While the ice cream mix is cooling, line a baking tray with a silicone mat and make the honeycomb.

Spread the sugar over the base of a saucepan then add the honey and 1 tablespoon of water. Bring to the boil whilst stirring gently to allow the sugar to dissolve.

Once the temperature reaches 150°C (300°F), quickly add the bicarbonate of soda and whisk until it is just mixed in. Do not overmix.

Swiftly pour the foaming syrup on to the prepared baking tray. Do not spread or disturb it, as this will cause it to deflate. Let it stand until cool to the touch – about 10 minutes.

Break into pieces and transfer immediately to an airtight container to preserve the crispness.

To use the honeycomb, scatter a handful of small pieces into the ice-cream maker 5 minutes before the end of the churning time; alternatively, ripple through once the ice cream is churned.

Serve with the toasted almonds and more honeycomb pieces.

TIRAMISU AND MOCHA RIPPLE ICE CREAM

We were asked to make this flavour for someone's ice cream birthday cake and they absolutely adored it, so we decided to sell this flavour combination in the shop for all our customers to enjoy. We do many variations depending on how we are feeling. Add Chocolate and Hazelnut Toffee Crunch (see page 150), for extra texture. You can also mix it with layers of Chocolate or Vanilla Ice Cream (see page 28 and 36).

800 ml (27 fl oz) Basic Sweetened Ice Cream Mix (see page 14)

40 ml (1½ fl oz) Kahlua or similar coffee-flavoured liqueur

30 ml (1 fl oz) dark rum

to serve

2–3 tablespoons Mocha Ripple (see page 141)

Make one quantity of the basic sweetened mix. Leave to cool.

Whisk together the coffee-flavoured liqueur and rum then add to the cooled base mix. Place in an ice-cream maker and churn.

Remove the ice cream from the machine and layer it into a container, gently rippling it through with the mocha ripple.

Scoop the churned ice cream into a container and keep in the freezer until ready to serve.

RUM AND RAISIN ICE CREAM

Our male customers love this combined with Salted Caramel Ice Cream *(see page 48)*. The finely chopped orange zest adds another layer to the flavour.

---

for the ice cream

800 ml (27 fl oz)
Basic Unsweetened Ice
Cream Mix *(see page 15)*

2 tablespoons
agave nectar
(see suppliers page 152)

for the rum and raisin

250 g (9 oz)
mixed raisins, sultanas
or currants

300 ml (10 fl oz)
dark or golden rum

3 strips
orange peel,
approximately 2cm
(¾ in) wide

3 tablespoons
orange zest

Make one quantity of the basic unsweetened mix and prepare to the stage before cooling.

Add the agave nectar to the hot ice cream mix and mix well. Remove from the heat and cool down. When cold, keep in the fridge for up to 3 days.

Place the raisins, rum and orange peel in a saucepan, bring to the boil and simmer for 2 minutes, then remove from heat, cool and leave to marinate overnight in the fridge.

Drain the raisins in a sieve over a measuring jug, discard the peel, but keep the rum liquid in the jug and the raisins in a bowl.

The rum liquid needs to measure about 100 ml (3½ fl oz); if necessary, add more rum. Stir into the mix, along with half of the raisins and half of the orange zest.

When you are ready to add the rum and raisins to the ice cream, place the mix in the ice-cream maker and churn.

Remove the ice cream from your machine and layer it into a container, interspersed with the rest of the raisins and orange zest. This will prevent them all being squashed and the whole mix turning brown.

VANILLA ICE CREAM

People often judge your ice cream by the quality of the vanilla that you produce. This one is seemingly simple, but complex in its range of flavours. We use the highest quality Madagascan vanilla pods – they are not grown in North London, but nevertheless sourced from family-run farms in Madagascar.

800 ml (27 fl oz)
Basic Sweetened Ice
Cream Mix (see page 14)

2 vanilla pods,
split lengthwise and
seeds scraped out
(use the pod and seeds)

1 teaspoon
pure vanilla powder,
made from crushed
Madagascan vanilla pods

Make one quantity of the basic sweetened mix and make up to the stage before cooling.

Add the vanilla pods and vanilla powder to the hot sweetened mix, then whisk together and leave to cool.

Keep in the fridge and leave for 6 hours or preferably overnight.

Remove the vanilla pods, making sure that you scrape out any mix inside the pods.

Churn in an ice-cream maker and then scoop into a container. Keep in the freezer until ready to serve.

Variation

Seville Orange Marmalade Ripple Ice Cream

Make the vanilla ice cream as above, then when the mix has been churned, ripple it with Seville Orange Marmalade (see page 139). You could also try using Raspberry Ripple (see page 137).

MINT CHOCOLATE CHIP
ICE CREAM

Our mint is supplied by our customers from their allotments in Highgate, so is completely fresh and natural. Do not be surprised if your mint chocolate ice cream does not turn out the fluorescent green that is commonly associated with the industrially extruded variety. Depending on the mint, the colour will vary from pale green to white, but the flavour will be unmistakable.

800 ml (27 fl oz)
Basic Sweetened Ice
Cream Mix (see page 14)

40 g (1½ oz)
mint leaves stripped
from the stalks

100 g (3½ oz)
chocolate (at least 60%
cocoa solids)

Make one quantity of the basic sweetened mix and prepare to the stage before cooling.

Add the mint leaves to the hot sweetened mix.

Leave to cool, then place in the fridge and leave for 6 hours or preferably overnight. The longer you can leave the mix, the more intense the flavour, as long as it is kept in the fridge and the ingredients are fresh. We leave ours to infuse for 2 days.

Strain the mix through a sieve, pressing the mint leaves firmly to extract all the mix. You may need to make the quantity back up to 800 ml (27 fl oz) with pasteurised milk.

Pour the mix into the ice-cream maker and churn.

Melt the chocolate in a bain-marie and leave on one side to cool, but stir occasionally so it remains runny.

Remove the ice cream from the machine and layer it into a container, interspersed with dribbles of melted chocolate to form chocolate chips.

Keep in the freezer until ready to serve.

ORANGE AND CANDIED PEEL ICE CREAM

The great thing about making your ice cream straight from fresh fruit is the wonderful aroma that is produced. Our customers are regularly enticed to the kitchen door by the emerging fragrances. This takes some preparation and you need to make the candied orange peels (see page 128) before you make the ice cream.

800 ml (27 fl oz)
Basic Sweetened Ice
Cream Mix (see page 14)

350 ml (12fl oz)
orange juice
(approx 5–6 oranges)

25 g (1 oz)
candied orange peel,
chopped into 0.5 cm
(¼ in) pieces
(see page 128)

4 teaspoons
lemon juice

Make one quantity of the basic sweetened mix and prepare to the stage before cooling.

While the ice cream mix is cooling down, stir the orange juice in the pan over a high heat until it has reduced to 250 ml (8½ fl oz). Set aside to cool.

Stir the cold reduced juice, 10 g (½ oz) of orange candied peel and the lemon juice into the cold ice cream mix.

Keep in the fridge for up to 3 days before churning in an ice-cream maker. Remove the ice cream from your machine and layer it into a container, interspersed with the rest of candied orange peel. Keep in the freezer until ready to serve.

LEMON AND CARDAMOM
ICE CREAM

Cardamoms have been traded in India for over thousands of years, so it is no surprise that this ice cream was brought to my attention by one of my Indian friends. The colour of this ice cream is pale, but the delicate flavour is distinctly exotic.

800 ml (27 fl oz)
Basic Sweetened Ice
Cream Mix (see *page 14*)

I piece of lemon peel,
8 x 3 cm
(3¼ x 1¼ in)

I vanilla pod,
split lengthwise and
seeds scraped out
(use the pod and seeds)

I tablespoon
cardamom pods, crushed

I tablespoon lemon zest

50 ml (2 fl oz)
lemon juice

Make one quantity of the basic sweetened mix and prepare to the stage before cooling.

Add the lemon peel, vanilla pod and crushed cardamom to the hot sweetened mix. Leave to cool then leave to infuse in the fridge for 6 hours or preferably overnight.

Strain through a sieve to remove the lemon peel, vanilla pod and cardamom seeds. Stir the lemon zest and juice into the cold ice cream mix and pour into an ice-cream maker and churn.

Scoop the churned ice cream into a container and keep in the freezer until ready to serve.

LIQUORICE AND BLACKCURRANT RIPPLE

Do not bother with liquorice powder or root as they are just not strong enough. Use these liquorice pellets and if you are a lover of liquorice you will not be disappointed. I like really strong liquorice and am very happy to double the strength, but I suspect for most people 16 pellets will be enough. People seem to have a very strong reaction to this ice cream – some are addicted; others won't go near it!

---

800 ml (27 fl oz)
Basic Sweetened Ice
Cream Mix (see page 14)

16 Amarelli spezzata
liquorice pellets
(see suppliers page 152)

2–3 tablespoons
Blackcurrant Ripple
(see page 135)

Make one quantity of the basic sweetened mix and prepare to the stage before cooling.

Whisk the liquorice pellets into the hot ice cream mix until completely melted. Continue to stir at this temperature for 4 minutes or so.

Leave to cool, then pour into an ice-cream maker and churn.

Remove the ice cream from the machine and layer it into a container, gently rippling it through with the blackcurrant ripple.

Keep in the freezer until ready to serve.

PEANUT BUTTER AND STRAWBERRY RIPPLE ICE CREAM

For environmental reasons, I prefer to use a peanut butter that does not contain any palm oil, but I have yet to find an organic peanut butter with exactly the right texture suitable for this ice cream. The search goes on…

800 ml (27 fl oz)
Basic Sweetened Ice
Cream Mix (see page 14)

200 g (7 oz)
crunchy peanut butter

2–3 tablespoons
Strawberry Ripple
(see page 138)

Make one quantity of the basic sweetened mix and prepare to the stage before cooling.

Remove the hot ice cream mix from the heat and stir in the peanut butter. This needs to be well mixed.

Leave to cool. You can do this the night before and leave in the fridge.

Thoroughly stir the mix then pour into an ice-cream maker and churn.

Layer the ice cream into a container, gently rippling it through with the strawberry ripple.

Keep in the freezer until ready to serve.

CROPWELL BISHOP STILTON AND WHITE PORT ICE CREAM

The Stilton we use comes from Cropwell Bishop, a village in Nottinghamshire, 20 minutes down the road from where my parents live and is perfect for this recipe, but any good quality blue cheese will work too. I find that Niepoort white port is delicious and complements the creamy texture of the cheese, preventing it from becoming too heavy. This tastes great with a Pear Sorbet *(see page 80)*.

500 ml (17 fl oz) double cream

250 ml (8½ fl oz) whole milk

30 g (1 oz) granulated (raw) sugar

45 ml (1½ fl oz) egg yolk (approximately 3 large eggs)

pinch of salt

60 g (2 oz) Stilton cheese (this depends on the maturity of the cheese, you may need slightly more), rind removed and cut into 1 cm (½ in) cubes

1 clove

3 tablespoons white port

2 tablespoons lemon juice

Pour the cream, milk and sugar into a saucepan. Bring slowly to the boil then remove from the heat and allow to cool a little.

In a large bowl, whisk together the salt and egg yolks until thoroughly combined.

Slowly pour the slightly cooled milk and cream on to the egg mixture, stirring constantly. Do not use boiling milk as this can turn your egg mixture into scrambled eggs.

Pour the mixture back into the pan and slowly heat, stirring with a wooden spoon continuously, until it has reached 85°C (185°F).

Stir at this temperature for 4 minutes or so. Do not allow it to boil.

Add the cubed Stilton to the saucepan and stir over a low to medium heat until it has all melted. Remove from the heat.

Add the clove and the port, then taste and season with lemon juice, plus a little salt or pepper if necessary.

Cool down to 4°C (39°F) within 90 minutes. To do this, either place the mix in a pan in a sink with cold water and ice cubes, or put the mix in a Ziploc bag inside a pan of cold water with ice cubes.

Remove the clove and pour the mixture into an ice-cream maker and churn. Scoop the churned ice cream into a container and keep in the freezer until ready to serve.

As an alternative to the typical cheese board, serve on cheese biscuits with Pear Sorbet *(see page 80)* or grapes.

RICE PUDDING ICE CREAM

My grandma used to make rice pudding in an oblong enamel basin. My sister and I would argue over who would eat the skin, and scrape the bowl out, both fiercely contested objectives. This ice cream goes well with Seville Orange Marmalade (see page 139).

**Makes 1 litre
(1¾ pints)**

800 ml (27 fl oz)
Basic Sweetened Ice
Cream Mix (see page 14)

75 g (2½ oz)
Italian Arborio rice

500 ml (17 fl oz)
whole milk

50 g (2 oz)
caster (superfine) sugar

¼ teaspoon
salt

1 vanilla pod

3 strips of orange zest,
each 2.5 cm
(1 in) wide

60 ml (2 fl oz)
egg yolks
(approximately 4 large
eggs; save the whites for
use later)

175 ml (6 fl oz)
double cream

pinch of freshly
grated nutmeg

Make one quantity of the basic sweetened mix and prepare to the stage before cooling.

While the ice cream base mix is cooling, make the rice pudding.

Preheat the oven to 170°C (340°F/Gas 3). In a baking dish, mix together the rice, milk, 20 g (¾ oz) of the sugar and the salt. Split the vanilla pod in half lengthwise and scrape out the seeds, then add both, plus strips of orange zest, to the baking dish.

Cover the dish with aluminum foil and bake for 45 minutes. Remove the rice from the oven and take off the foil. Stir in the remaining sugar, then continue to bake the rice, uncovered, for another 20 minutes.

Remove the rice from the oven, pick out the vanilla pods and orange zest and briskly whisk in the egg yolks all at once. Then whisk in the cream and nutmeg.

Purée half of the rice mixture in a food processor until the texture is fine then stir it back into the cooked rice.

Add 500 g (1 lb 2 oz) of the rice pudding to 300 ml (10 fl oz) of the sweetened base mix and churn in an ice-cream maker.

Reserve the rest of the sweetened base mix for another flavour, or just churn on its own as plain ice cream (Fior di Latte).

Scoop the churned ice cream into a container and keep in the freezer until ready to serve.

SALTED CARAMEL ICE CREAM

On our opening day at the market an American lady suggested an ice cream that she loved from a restaurant in Paris. After some experimentation we decided upon this recipe and it has remained a firm favourite ever since, with a fanatical following.

I like to use *Fleur de sel* salt for the salted caramel mix as it imparts a very partiular flavour and intensity. This recipe will make slightly more than will fit in your machine, so use the leftover ice cream for another recipe. You can serve this ice cream with Almond Nut Brittle (*see page 144*).

---

for the salted caramel mix

100 g (3½ oz)
granulated (raw) sugar

1 tablespoon
agave nectar
(*see suppliers page 152*)

120 ml (4 fl oz)
double cream

1 teaspoon
Fleur de sel salt

60 ml (2 fl oz)
soured cream
(made with 40 ml/1½ fl oz
double cream and
4 teaspoons lemon juice)

for the ice cream

800 ml (27 fl oz) Basic
Unsweetened Ice Cream
Mix (*see page 15*)

to serve

a few chunks of Almond
Nut Brittle (*see page 144*)

2–3 tablespoons of *Fleur
de sel* Caramel Sauce
(*see page 142*)

First make the salted caramel mix. Heat the sugar, agave nectar and 60 ml (2 fl oz) water in a medium-sized saucepan with a sugar thermometer. Stir to dissolve the sugar as you bring to the boil over a high heat.

Meanwhile, heat the cream and salt in another saucepan until the salt has dissolved and the cream has come to a boil, then remove and set aside.

Continue to heat the sugar mix until it reaches 180°C (350°F). It should be quite dark, just on the verge of being burnt. Remove from the heat and let it sit for a moment. Whisk the hot cream and salt into the hot sugar mix. It will spit as you do this, so take care and be careful it doesn't bubble up over the edge of the pan. As it is extremely hot, it may be better to place the pan in the bottom of a stainless-steel sink.

Whisk in the soured cream then leave to cool and store in the fridge.

To make the ice cream, make one quantity of the basic unsweetened mix and prepare to the stage before cooling.

When both mixtures are cool, mix them together and churn in an ice-cream maker.

After churning, transfer to a container and layer with Almond Nut Brittle if you wish. We like to serve ours with an extra layer of *Fleur de sel Caramel* Sauce for added flavour.

Keep in the freezer until ready to serve.

CHRISTMAS AND MARZIPAN ICE CREAM

For this ice cream I usually make a Christmas cake and get my son to decorate it. However if you don't have the time or a willing offspring to help, then it's fine to buy one; just make sure it's a rich, heavy fruit cake with good, wholesome ingredients. You don't need the cake to be iced for this recipe. Take the extra marzipan mix in this recipe and churn to make a delicious ice cream in its own right.

---

for the marzipan mix

800 ml (27 fl oz)
Basic Sweetened Ice
Cream Mix (see page 14)

200 g (7 oz)
white marzipan, cut into
2.5 cm (1 in) cubes

½ teaspoon
almond extract

½ teaspoon
salt

2 tablespoons
lemon juice

for the Christmas Ice Cream

800 ml (27 fl oz)
Basic Unsweetened Ice
Cream Mix (see page 14)

2 tablespoons
agave nectar
(see suppliers page 152)

100 ml (3½ fl oz)
marzipan mix

1 tablespoon
brandy

125 g (4 oz)
Christmas cake, diced
into roughly 1 cm
(½ inch) pieces

2 tablespoons
orange candied peel
(see page 128)

For the marzipan mix (you will only be using 100 ml (3.5 fl oz) of the mix in this recipe), make one quantity of the basic sweetened mix up to the point when it has reached 85°C (185°F). Add the cubed marzipan to the pan and over a low to medium heat stir until it has all melted. Remove from the heat.

Add the almond extract, salt and lemon juice and leave to cool. Keep in the fridge and leave to infuse for 6 hours or preferably overnight.

To make the Christmas ice cream, make one quantity of the basic unsweetened mix and prepare to the stage before cooling.

Remove the mix from the heat and stir in the agave nectar. Leave to cool, then add 100 ml (4 fl oz) of the cooled marzipan mix.

Take 30 g (1 oz) of the Christmas cake and crumble into the mix and churn. Pour in the brandy and churn in an ice-cream maker.

The rest of the Christmas cake and the candied peel should be layered into the ice cream after it has been churned and as you are spreading it into the container to go in the freezer. If you place it all in the ice cream before churning you will end up with a sludgy brown ice cream.

Keep in the freezer until you are ready to serve. We serve ours as a Christmas ball with a Brandy Parfait ball centre (see page 107).

Sorbets

I love standing behind my ice cream counter watching children's reactions to the the vivid and exotic colours of the sorbets: they seem drawn to them as if to jewels in a treasure chest. Like a jewel, a sorbet has a purity and intensity. It reflects the light enticingly, and there is a crystal clarity to the flavour. Our sorbets offer a delightful alternative to our dairy-based ice creams and are always popular with adults for their light and refreshing qualities, or with a wafer and a cone for an adventurous child. Each sorbet recipe makes approximately 1 litre (1¾ pints), unless otherwise stated.

Sorbets

BLACKCURRANT AND RASPBERRY SORBET

Not surprisingly this recipe is a favourite among little girls! The recipe works with frozen as well as fresh blackcurrants and raspberries. The taste and colour are intense and make all your foraging endeavours worthwhile. For the raspberry sorbet, removing the pips is a laborious process, so if you don't mind them, you need not bother with the sieving.

---

for the glucose syrup

75 g (2½ oz)
caster (superfine) sugar

15 g (½ oz)
glucose powder

15 g (½ oz)
lemon zest

4 teaspoons
lemon juice
(juice of about
half a lemon)

for the blackcurrant
sorbet mixture

600 g (1 lb 5 oz)
frozen blackcurrants

120 ml (4 fl oz)
sugar syrup
(see page 17)

for the raspberry
sorbet mixture

800 g (1 lb 12 oz)
fresh or frozen raspberries

200 ml (7 fl oz)
sugar syrup
(see page 17)

60 ml (2 fl oz)
lemon juice

To make the glucose syrup, put the caster sugar, glucose and 200 ml (7 fl oz) water in a saucepan with a thermometer. Stir and slowly heat up to 40°C (104°F) then continue heating to 85°C (185°F). Remove from the heat.

Add the lemon zest and juice to the hot glucose syrup and leave to infuse for 30 minutes.

For the blackcurrant sorbet mix, place the blackcurrants in a non-reactive pan with the sugar syrup and 600 ml (20 fl oz) water. Cover the pan, bring to the boil and simmer for 5 minutes.

Cool a little before pressing through a nylon sieve to remove the pips. Do not blitz in a food processor as the pips will give the sorbet a bitter taste.

Add the glucose syrup and stir to combine. Cool and refrigerate for 6 hours or preferably overnight. Once chilled, churn in an ice-cream maker.

To make the raspberry sorbet, purée all the ingredients together in a food processor. Strain through a fine sieve to remove the pips (optional), then churn.

Spoon the churned sorbets into your chosen serving dishes or freeze until needed. Remove 20 minutes before eating so that it is soft enough.

BLOOD ORANGE SORBET

There are a few varieties of Sicilian blood orange, but we prefer to use the Moro oranges which have a deep red colour. Customers ask for this sorbet more than any other, and it's very popular for weddings.

---

600 ml (20 fl oz)
blood orange juice
(approximately
8 oranges)

45 g (1½ oz)
icing (confectioners')
sugar

3 tablespoons
blood orange zest

5 teaspoons
lemon juice

90 ml (3 fl oz)
glucose syrup
(see page 17)

Pour the blood orange juice into a bowl then whisk in the icing sugar, either with an electric whisk or by hand.

Add half the blood orange zest, plus the lemon juice and the glucose syrup.

Refrigerate for 6 hours or preferably overnight before churning in an ice-cream maker.

Spoon the churned sorbet into a container until ready to serve or freeze until needed, removing it 20 minutes before serving so it can soften a little.

Sprinkle the remaining zest over the top to serve.

LIME SORBET

This is not a flavour for the faint-hearted as it is extremely tart and tangy. Best eaten sitting down!

---

500 ml (17 fl oz)
lime juice,
(approximately 12 limes
strained through a sieve
into a bowl to remove
any pips and pith)

1 star anise

100 ml (3½ fl oz)
glucose syrup
(see page 17)

2 tablespoons
lime zest

1 tablespoon
finely ground
Sichuan pepper

200 ml (7 fl oz)
sugar syrup
(see page 17)

Pour the lime juice into a bowl. Add the star anise, glucose syrup, lime zest and Sichuan pepper and stir to combine.

Refrigerate for 6 hours or preferably overnight.

When ready to churn, remove the mixture from the fridge, discard the star anise, then add the sugar syrup and 250 ml (8½ fl oz) water.

Pour into an ice-cream maker and churn.

Spoon the churned sorbet into a container until ready to serve or freeze until needed, removing it 20 minutes before serving so it can soften a little.

LEMON SORBET

In an ideal world we would choose Amalfi lemons for our sorbet, but these can be difficult to obtain. There is something special about this ancient fruit and its ties to the land and culture along the Amalfi coast are deep. We use every part of this noble knobbly fruit: the zest, the rind and the juice. The flavour is a real eyebrow raiser and many of our customers have suggested serving it with vodka.

500 ml (17 fl oz)
lemon juice
(approximately 12 lemons),
strained through a sieve
into a bowl to remove
pips and any pith

2 tablespoons
lemon zest

200 ml (7 fl oz)
glucose syrup
(see page 17)

200 ml (7 fl oz)
sugar syrup
(see page 17)

Mix the lemon juice, lemon zest and glucose syrup together in a bowl. Refrigerate for 6 hours or preferably overnight.

When ready to churn, remove the mixture from the fridge, add the sugar syrup, and churn in an ice-cream maker.

Spoon the churned sorbet into a container or freeze until ready to serve, removing it 20 minutes before serving so that it can soften a little.

PEACH AND ROSEWATER SORBET

In stark contrast to the powerful Lime Sorbet on page 58, Peach and Rosewater is an extremely delicate and fragrant sorbet. The colour comes from the peach skins and is a perfect pairing with the Blackcurrant Sorbet *(see page 56)*.

1 kg (2.2 lb)
(approximately
8 fruits)

250 ml (8½ fl oz)
glucose syrup
(see page 17)

180 ml (6 fl oz)
sugar syrup
(see page 17)

2 tablespoons
rosewater
(I use Mymoune brand, see suppliers page 152)

50 ml (2 fl oz)
lemon juice
(approximately
1 lemon)

Wipe clean and dry the peaches. Cut into quarters, remove the stones then purée the peaches, with the skins on, in a blender.

Push the peach juice through a sieve – this will yield approx 400 ml (13 fl oz) purée.

Blend together the peach purée, glucose syrup, sugar syrup, rosewater and lemon juice then refrigerate for 6 hours or preferably overnight.

Once chilled, churn in an ice-cream maker. Spoon the churned sorbet into a container or freeze until ready to serve, removing it from the freezer 20 minutes before serving so it can soften a little.

SEVILLE ORANGE SORBET

Seville oranges are too bitter to eat on their own, but in a sorbet they work really well. This sorbet is very different from Blood Orange Sorbet *(see page 58)* in terms of taste and colour, as it's much tangier and paler.

---

8 Seville oranges

1 lemon

650 ml (22 fl oz) sugar syrup *(see page 17)*

Wash and dry the oranges. Take 2 of the oranges and carefully zest in thin strips. Grate fine zest from another 2 oranges so you end up with different sizes and textures in the finished sorbet.

Cut the oranges and lemon in half and juice them all together. Stir the juice and sugar syrup. Add all the zest and refrigerate for 6 hours or preferably overnight.

Pour into an ice-cream maker and churn. The zest helps the sorbet freeze, so don't remove it.

Spoon the churned sorbet into a container, or freeze until needed, removing it 20 minutes before serving so that it can soften a little.

GIN AND TONIC SORBET

Use good-quality gin and tonic such as Bombay Sapphire with Fever Tree tonic. As with any sorbet made with alcohol, this one requires a cold freezer and to be stored carefully as over time the alcohol will separate out. Best eaten straight away.

150 ml (5 fl oz)
gin

500 ml (17 fl oz)
sugar syrup
(see page 17)

45 ml (1½ fl oz)
lemon juice (1 lemon)

400 ml (13 fl oz)
tonic water

Combine the gin, sugar syrup and lemon juice in a bowl and refrigerate for 6 hours or preferably overnight.

Meanwhile, place the bottle of tonic water in the fridge to get cold.

When the sorbet mixture is ready, take it out of the fridge and add the cold tonic water, pour into an ice-cream maker and churn immediately.

Spoon the churned sorbet into a container or freeze until needed, removing it 20 minutes before serving so that it can soften a little. However, I do recommend that you eat this sorbet as soon as possible.

MOJITO GRANITA

Mojito cocktails are popular because they combine the sweetness of sugar with the astringency of mint leaves and the citrus kick of limes, all of which are recreated here in this refreshing granita. These go down a treat in the summer and especially when we have 'Happy Hour' in our parlour.

500 g (1 lb 2 oz/2¼ cups) caster (superfine) sugar

zest of 3 limes

80 g (3 oz) mint leaves

170 ml (6 fl oz) lime juice (approximately 4 limes)

60 ml (2 fl oz) white rum

Mix the sugar with 500 ml (17 fl oz) water in a saucepan, then add the lime zest and bring it to the boil. Once the sugar has dissolved, add 50 g (2 oz) of the mint leaves and remove from the heat. Cover and leave to stand until cool.

Once cool, refrigerate for 2–3 hours for the mint to infuse.

Strain the chilled syrup through a sieve to remove the mint leaves.

Stir in the lime juice along with the rum. Finely chop the remaining mint and add.

To make a granita, pour the mixture into a shallow metal tray and put into the freezer. Every 3 hours, remove and break up the ice crystals with a fork, until ready to serve.

Alternatively, to make into a sorbet, churn in your ice-cream maker.

POMEGRANATE SORBET

In my experience Peruvian pomegranates are best for this sorbet as they give the richest colour and the deepest flavour, and they are not overly sweet. Ensure that the pomegranates are fully ripened and the skin has thinned and dried from a thick pithy coat. The challenge of always using fresh fruit is maintaining consistency, and nowhere is this more critical than with pomegranates.

Makes 1.1 litres
(2 pints)

5 pomegranates

225 ml (8 fl oz)
sugar syrup
(see page 17)

45 ml (1½ fl oz)
lemon juice

pinch of salt

Wash the pomegranates thoroughly and pat dry.

Cut the pomegranates in half and juice the seeds using a glass juicer or the electric equivalent. I would avoid using a fruit juicer as the pith may be incorporated into the flavour.

Put the remaining seeds in a sieve and squish using a wooden spoon or spatula, to extract as much juice as you can. You are aiming to extract 900 ml (30 fl oz) juice.

Mix the pomegranate juice, sugar syrup, lemon juice and salt in a bowl and refrigerate for 6 hours or preferably overnight.

When ready, pour into an ice-cream maker and churn. Spoon the churned sorbet into a container, or freeze until needed, removing it 20 minutes before serving so that it can soften a little.

WATERMELON GRANITA

This is a lovely refreshing, summery granita. To choose the perfect watermelon, it should sound hollow and have a yellow or light bottom. Many melons in supermarkets are picked unripe so it's best to check before buying.

---

60 ml (2 fl oz)
sugar syrup
(see page 17)

500 ml (17 fl oz)
watermelon juice

50 ml (2 fl oz)
lemon juice
(1 lemon)

100 ml (3½ fl oz)
honey

5 mint leaves,
finely chopped

Chop the flesh of approximately a quarter of an average-sized watermelon. Purée in a food processor and strain through a fine sieve to remove the pips, then measure out 500 ml (17 fl oz) juice.

Pour the juice back into the food processor, add the sugar syrup, lemon juice and honey and blend until well combined.

To make granita, pour the mixture, along with the mint leaves into a shallow metal tray and put into the freezer. Every 3 hours, remove and break up the ice crystals with a fork. Do this until you are ready to serve it.

Alternatively, to make into a sorbet, churn in your ice-cream maker.

CHOCOLATE SORBET

This sorbet is really popular and very chocolatey – a chocoholic's dream in fact! Dutch-processed (or alkalized) cocoa powder, which I've specified here, is treated with an alkaline to reduce the acidity of the cocoa, giving it a milder and smoother flavour and a darker colour. It's important that the cocoa you use is unsweetened.

175 g (6 oz/¾ cup) caster (superfine) sugar

60 g (2 oz) unsweetened Dutch-process cocoa powder

½ teaspoon salt

150 g (5 oz) chocolate (at least 60% cocoa solids), chopped into small pieces

½ teaspoon vanilla extract

Mix the sugar, cocoa powder and salt with 350 ml (12 fl oz) water in a large saucepan. Continually whisking, bring to the boil and keep boiling for 1 minute.

Remove the pan from the heat, stir in the chocolate then, when it has completely melted, add the vanilla extract and a further 150 ml (5 fl oz) water.

Pour into a food processor and blend for 2–3 minutes until smooth. Once cool, refrigerate for 6 hours or preferably overnight. If the mixture has become too thick to pour into your ice-cream maker, whisk it vigorously to thin it out then pour into your ice-cream maker and churn.

When churned, spoon the sorbet into a container or freeze until ready to serve, removing it 20 minutes before serving so that it can soften a little.

MANGO AND PASSION FRUIT SORBET

Alphonso mangoes were shipped to England from Mumbai's teeming Crawford market for the coronation of Queen Elizabeth II. Now more widely available, they are the king of mangoes, sweet and delicious, but with a short season. The passion fruit should be slightly wrinkly so that they are still quite tart – the more wrinkled they are, the sweeter the fruit will be.

10–12 passion fruit
(to yield 200 ml
(7 fl oz) juice)

3–4 mangoes
(to yield 300 ml
(10 fl oz) juice)

200 ml (7 fl oz)
glucose syrup
(see page 17)

150 ml (5 fl oz)
sugar syrup
(see page 17)

75 ml (2½ fl oz)
lemon juice

To juice the passion fruit, cut them in half and scoop out the flesh and seeds into a food processor. Blend for 2 minutes and push through a sieve. All that should be left in the sieve are the black seeds; if there is still some flesh, whizz round in the food processor for a further minute or so.

Next peel and slice the mangoes. Put the mango slices in the food processor and blend until you have a smooth purée, then push it through a sieve.

Blend the passion fruit purée, mango purée, glucose syrup, sugar syrup and lemon juice together. Once blended, refrigerate for 6 hours or preferably overnight.

Once chilled, pour into an ice-cream maker and churn.

Spoon the churned sorbet it into a container or freeze until needed, removing it 20 minutes before serving so that it can soften a little.

MULLED WINE SORBET

Inevitably this sorbet is very popular around Christmas and New Year. It will enliven you after the heaviest of Christmas dinners. The sorbet is inspired by a recipe from Caroline and Robin Weir's book *Ices*.

---

150 g (5 oz/¼ cup) caster (superfine) sugar

2 clementines

1 lemon

1 lime

2 cloves

1 star anise

3 cardamom pods, crushed

1 cinnamon stick

350 ml (12fl oz) red wine

1 teaspoon grated nutmeg

1 small thumb-sized piece of fresh root ginger

40 ml (1½ fl oz) ruby port

Put the sugar in a pan with 200 ml (7 fl oz) water, then bring to the boil and simmer, stirring to dissolve the sugar. Set the sugary syrup on one side.

Rinse and dry the clementines, lemon and lime. Remove 6 pieces of clementine peel and 2 pieces of lemon and lime peel – approximately 8 x 3 cm (3 x 1½ in) – with a vegetable peeler. Each piece of peel should then be cut into about 30 very fine strips.

Juice the clementines, lemons and lime, keep the clementine pulp (if there is any) and pour into a saucepan.

Wrap the cloves, star anise, crushed cardamom pods and cinnamon stick in a muslin bag and add to the pan with any clementine pulp, the wine, strips of peel, grated nutmeg and ginger.

Bring to the boil and simmer for 2 minutes, then remove from the heat. Leave to cool and infuse for 2 hours, then remove the muslin bag, ginger and strips of peel.

Sieve to remove the fruit pulp, returning the strips of peel to the mixture. This helps the sorbet freeze, so don't remove it.

Stir in the port and sugar syrup then pour into an ice-cream maker and churn.

Spoon the churned sorbet into a container or freeze until needed, removing it 20 minutes before serving so that it can soften a little.

PEAR SORBET

Much commercial forced fruit production diminishes a strong and individual flavour, which means that the fresher and more local pears are the better. We use a number of different varieties such as Comice, Conference and Bartlett as we tend to go on their flavour rather than any specific rule as to which is better. Pear sorbet has a strong and faithful following, and our customers have carried it far beyond the boundaries of North London with an evangelical zeal.

---

1 kg (2 lb 3oz)
pears

80 ml (2½ fl oz)
sugar syrup
(see page 17)

2 vanilla pods,
split lengthwise and seeds
scraped out, but use the
pod and seeds

1 star anise

120 ml (4 fl oz)
lemon juice

150 ml (5 fl oz)
glucose syrup
(see page 17)

Peel the pears, remove the core and cut each one into 6.

Bring the sugar syrup to the boil in a saucepan. Reduce to a simmer then add the pears, the vanilla pods and star anise to the pan. Simmer for 15 minutes or so until the fruit is soft.

Remove the star anise and vanilla pods and set to one side.

Liquidise the pears and syrup, add the lemon juice, then return the star anise and vanilla pods to the pear mixture. Leave to cool then add the glucose syrup.

Mix together and leave in the refrigerator for 6 hours or preferably overnight

Remove the star anise and vanilla pods before pouring into an ice- cream maker and churn.

Spoon the churned sorbet into a container or freeze until needed, removing it 20 minutes before serving so that it can soften a little.

This compliments Stilton and white port perfectly or Rhubarb and Strawberry sorbet (see page 82).

BLOODY MARY SORBET

One of our customers serves this with Sweet Basil Ice Cream (see *page 26*) as a starter.

---

50 g (2 oz)
caster (superfine)
sugar

600 ml (20 fl oz)
tomato juice

3 tablespoons
vodka

juice of 1 lime

½ tablespoon
Tabasco sauce

Put the sugar into a saucepan with 75 ml (2½ fl oz) water. Bring to the boil, then turn down the heat and simmer until slightly thicker and syrupy. Remove the sugary syrup from the heat and cool completely.

Mix the cooled syrup with all the other ingredients in a bowl and refrigerate for 6 hours or preferably overnight.

When ready, pour the mixture in an ice-cream maker and churn.

Spoon the churned sorbet into a container, or freeze until needed, removing it 20 minutes before serving so that it can soften a little.

QUINCE AND MOSCATO D'ASTI SORBET

Quince is a lovely old-fashioned fruit. Not usually eaten raw, it makes a lovely aromatic sorbet. Our kitchen is filled with its divine perfume, which lingers long in the memory.

---

4 British quinces

250 g (9 oz/1 cup)
caster (superfine) sugar

1 vanilla pod

200 ml (7 fl oz)
Moscato D'Asti

5 teaspoons
lemon juice
(approximately half
a lemon)

pinch of salt

Place the whole quinces in a pan with the sugar, vanilla pod and wine. Cover with foil and cook on a very low heat for 3½–4 hours until they're really soft and a burnt-orange colour.

Cool, liquidise and purée through a sieve. Add the lemon juice and salt. and pour into an ice-cream maker and churn immediately.

Spoon the churned sorbet into a container or freeze until needed, removing it from the freezer 20 minutes before serving so that it can soften a little.

RHUBARB AND STRAWBERRY SORBET

From January to March we source forced rhubarb from the Yorkshire, but during the summer it comes direct from our customers' allotments. I can't remember how we came about combining these flavours, but this delicious sorbet certainly works well. We've served ours with a Pear Sorbet *(see page 80)*, as photographed.

12–15 sticks
rhubarb

650 g (1 lb 7 oz)
hulled strawberries

1 large
vanilla pod

90 g (3¼ oz / ⅓ cup)
caster (superfine) sugar

170 ml (6 fl oz)
glucose syrup
(see page 17)

130 ml (4fl oz)
sugar syrup
(see page 17)

2 teaspoons
lemon juice

Trim and peel the rhubarb, then chop into 5 cm (2 in) pieces and weigh out 480 g (1 lb 1 oz).

Place the rhubarb in a saucepan with the vanilla pod, sugar and 125 ml (4fl oz) water.

Bring to a simmer and cook gently for 5 minutes or so, stirring occasionally, until the sugar has dissolved. The rhubarb should be soft. Use a slotted spoon and transfer the rhubarb to a bowl.

Turn the heat up under the pan and boil until the liquid has reduced by half. Leave to cool.

In a food processor purée the rhubarb, glucose syrup, sugar syrup and lemon juice, the pan of reduced liquid and the hulled strawberries.

Refrigerate for 6 hours or preferably overnight. When ready pour the mixture into an ice-cream maker and churn.

Spoon the churned sorbet into a container or freeze until needed, removing it from the freezer 20 minutes before serving so that it can soften a little.

ELDERFLOWER AND PROSECCO SORBET

I collected elderflowers from nearby woodland when creating this sorbet — a very pleasant way to spend the morning but it was a time consuming process. If you choose to do this don't wash the elderflowers as it removes the pollen, but do remove the bitter-tasting stalks. For this recipe I have used an organic elderflower cordial.

35 ml (1 fl oz)
elderflower cordial

30 ml (1 fl oz)
glucose syrup
(see page 17)

330 ml (11 fl oz)
sugar syrup
(see page 17)

120 ml (4 fl oz)
lemon juice
(3–4 lemons)

pinch of salt

120 ml (4 fl oz)
Prosecco

Whisk together the elderflower cordial, glucose syrup, sugar syrup lemon juice and salt with 500 ml (17 fl oz) water in a bowl.

Refrigerate for 6 hours or preferably overnight. Meanwhile, place the bottle of Prosecco in the fridge to get really cold.

Once the sorbet is ready, take it out of the fridge and add the cold Prosecco then pour into an ice-cream maker and churn immediately.

Spoon the churned sorbet into a container or freeze until needed, removing it from the freezer 20 minutes before serving so that it can soften a little.

Special desserts

❖

Back in Victorian times, Mrs Agnes Marshall used tin-lined copper moulds to shape ice creams into a creative menagerie of doves and swans — even hens and fish adorned her table. With the more recent development of silicone moulds, the creative options are endless, as is the fun experimenting with them.

Remember, when presentation is important, the colder the freezer the better for that precise finish. The recipes in this chapter represent some of the ideas that have been successful at our shop, but the list is ever expanding. Each one uses a range of ice cream flavours, so all you have to do is pick your favourite and have fun creating these delectable desserts!

Special desserts

BAKED ALASKA

Our mini version of Baked Alaskas consists of a small ball of ice cream on top of a firm sponge disc coated in meringue. Use whichever flavour of ice cream you prefer, but we find that Vanilla with a Raspberry Ripple works best *(see pages 36 and 137)*.

Serves 6

**for the genoese
sponge base**

4 eggs

125 g (4 oz/½ cup)
caster (superfine) sugar

1 teaspoon
lemon zest

125 g (4 oz/1 cup)
plain flour (all-purpose),
sifted

125 g (4 oz/½ cup)
butter, melted and cooled

for the meringue topping

80 ml (2½ fl oz)
egg whites (approx 2–3)

¼ teaspoon
cream of tartar

¼ teaspoon
salt

90 g (3½ oz/scant ⅓ cup)
caster (superfine) sugar

6 small scoops/balls
of ice cream
(approximately
4 cm/1½ in across)

Preheat the oven to 170°C (340°F/Gas 3). Line a baking tray with baking parchment.

First make the sponge base. Whisk the eggs and sugar in a bain-marie over a medium heat, until the mixture becomes light and creamy. When the volume has increased by about 50% and the mixture is thick enough to hold a ribbon trail, remove from the heat and transfer to a large mixing bowl.

Add the lemon zest then, using a large metal spoon, carefully fold the sifted flour into the mix alternately with in the melted butter.

Pour the mixture quickly on to the lined baking tray and bake for 20 minutes.

Leave to cool then cut out 6 discs with a 5 cm (2 in) round cutter and place on baking parchment or on a silicone mat on a baking tray.

To make the meringue, slowly whisk the egg whites in a food processor, until frothy. Add the cream of tartar and the salt and whisk until you have soft peaks.

Heat the sugar in a saucepan with 2 tablespoons water until it reaches a temperature of 116°C (240°F), then remove from the heat.

While slowly whisking the egg whites, dribble the sugar syrup down the side of the food processor bowl, avoiding the whisk. Then briskly whisk for 2–3 minutes until you have glossy, firm peaks. The mix should be elastic but firm.

To assemble the dessert, place a scoop of ice cream on top of each sponge disc. Totally coat the ice cream and the sponge base with the meringue and freeze for 4–6 hours. The Alaskas will keep in the freezer for up to 2 days.

Preheat the oven to 240°C (450°F/Gas 8) and bake on a silicone mat for 5–10 minutes, testing one on it's own first. The Baked Alaskas should be firm and crisp on the outside and frozen in the middle.

RUBY'S ANTARCTIC ROLL

This is particularly good made with Orange Ice Cream *(see page 40)* or Mint Chocolate Chip Ice Cream *(see page 38)*.

Serves 8

800 ml–1 litre
(27 fl oz–1¾ pints)
Ice cream

4 eggs

125 g (4 oz/½ cup)
sugar

100 g (3½ oz/scant 1 cup)
self-raising flour

20 g (¾ oz)
cocoa powder, sieved

1 pinch of salt

Churn your ice cream of choice, then use baking parchment, clingfilm or a silicone mat, carefully roll the ice cream into a sausage shape, 5–6 cm (2–2½ in) in diameter. The length of the ice cream sausage should be same as the width of the tray for your chocolate sponge.

Once it's rolled, put the ice cream, still wrapped up, in the freezer for an hour to firm up.

Preheat the oven to 170°C (340°F/Gas 3).

Place the eggs and sugar in a food processor and whisk until very light, fluffy and thickened. Sift the flour over the mixture and fold in with the cocoa and salt, carefully.

Line your tray (20 x 30 x 3 cm/8 x 12 x 1¼ in) with baking parchment or a silicone mat. Pour the mixture onto the lined tray and smooth with a spatula until evenly spread out.

Bake the sponge for 10–12 minutes. Leave the sponge in the tray to cool, and cover with a clean tea towel.

Once the Swiss roll is cool, take out of the tin and peel away the baking paper or silicone mat. Flip it face down on to a clean sheet of baking paper.

Remove the wrapper from the ice cream and place your ice cream sausage on the sponge. Wrap the cool sponge around the ice cream, trim the ends off.

Wrap in baking parchment and put back in the freezer for an hour or until you need to serve it. Dust the top with sieved cocoa powder before serving.

ICE CREAM CAKES

You can have as many flavours and layers as you like in this kind of ice cream 'cake', but remember that the flavours with ripples will melt more quickly than those without. Don't mix sorbets with ice creams as they may well melt at different speeds. My favourite combination is a base of Salted Caramel *(see page 48)* with a Chocolate centre *(see page 28)* and a mint ice cream to top it off *(see page 38)*, as pictured.

Churn the ice cream of your choice, but remove it before it is too hard. Pour into a silicone cake mould – we use one that is 16 cm (6½ in) wide. The depth of each layer is up to you – our layers are usually about 1.5–2 cm (½–¾ in) deep, but it can be really pretty to vary the sizes.

There are two ways to make up the cake. You can either make a layer, freeze it, then pour the next layer on top and repeat, but the layers will not be as sharp. If you have more than one mould, you can make the layers simultaneously depending on the freezer space available and type of ice-cream maker you have.

If you make the layers individually then you will need a large spatula or cake slice to seal them together. To do this, remove the layers from the freezer and heat the spatula with some boiling water, then thoroughly dry it. If you leave the spatula wet then there will be ice between the layers.

Place the bottom layer of the cake on a board (covered with a silicone mat, baking parchment or greaseproof paper). With the hot spatula, melt the top of this layer and the next layer. As the ice cream starts to soften, join the layers together. Once all the layers are joined, cover with waxed paper and another board. Placing a board on top, with weight, can help to join the layers together and stop them from seperating once the cake is cut. Return to the freezer.

Once your cake is assembled place on a cake board and decorate with fresh fruit (raspberries work very well) or as I have done, with Almond Nut Brittle *(see page 144)*. For an extra wow factor, swirl some melted and cooled chocolate onto the base of the silicone mould before pouring in the mix and placing it in the freezer. You can tie a ribbon around the outside for extra effect.

GELOLLIES

These are simple to do and the possibilities are endless. Silicone moulds are available in an array of sizes and shapes, with the wooden sticks to fit. Some moulds come with a tray – if not, use a freezerproof board.

Choose your flavour and churn your ice cream. It needs to be a fairly thick consistency, but not so solid that you have to push it into the mould. If the consistency is too runny it will seep out of the hole where the stick goes and if too solid the shape will not be smooth.

If you are using a ripple, be sparing with it when making the ice cream as this will not freeze. If you are using the Salted Caramel (see page 48) it works really well if you put a small spoonful of the Fleur de sel Caramel Sauce (see page 142) in the middle. Be neat filling the moulds and wipe across with a spatula to get a really smooth finish. Always add your ripples or toppings before freezing.

You can also sprinkle fine nut brittle or drizzled melted and cooled chocolate in a pattern across the bottom of the mould before filling it.

Once your ice creams are frozen, you can unmould them and dip in chocolate, or drizzle chocolate over them, pretty much whatever you fancy.

It is much easier to keep them frozen when decorating if you have them on a tray that has also been in the freezer.

NEAPOLITAN

If you want a topping such as Candied Citrus Peel or Almond Nut Brittle *(see pages 128 and 144)* embedded in the ice cream, add before putting your first layer of ice cream in the mould. Decide what flavour you would like at the top. We used Orange and Candied Peel *(see page 40)*, with raspberry ripple ice cream in the centre and pistachio at the bottom. These look so pretty, and taste delicious – the variations are endless.

To make your Neapolitan, take your top layer ice cream and gently spread it evenly with a spatula across the base of a 20 x 10 cm (8 x 4 in) silicone loaf mould.

Place in the freezer until hard enough to put another layer on top (2–3 hours). Repeat the steps until you have your three layers. Leave, preferably overnight, to allow the whole block to freeze well. Remove from the mould and add any further decoration.

ICE CREAM BLOCKS

These are a real favourite at Ruby Violet's and are really easy to make. Once again, they can be made using any flavoured ice cream of your choice. I suggest adding a rippled flavour to your ice cream, for extra taste and elegance. Try eating them with Wafers (see page 146), or you can buy ready made ones. They can be coated in chocolate and dipped in nuts — again, the possibilities are endless!

These blocks are made by layering ice cream into a silicone mould and then running a ripple through it.

You can find silicone mould on the Internet; ours are Italian, and just the right shape and size measuring at 10 x 6 cm (4 x 2½ in) to create a small block of ice cream. Slide between 2 wafers for an added texture and crunch!

MILKSHAKES

A favourite with adults and kids alike, our milkshakes are not only simple to make, but also a delight to your taste buds. Vanilla with Raspberry Ripple *(see pages 36 and 137)* is popular amongst our customers, but feel free to experiment with different flavour combinations.

Makes 1

250 ml (8½ fl oz) whole milk

2 scoops ice cream

Pour the milk into a liquidiser or use an electric whisk, followed by the ice cream. Blend thoroughly. Pour into a tall glass and swirl some of the ripple through.

Other flavour combinations that work well are White Chocolate and Toasted Coconut *(see page 27)* and Orange and Candied Peel *(see page 40).*

OAT AND RAISIN 'SANDWICH' BISCUITS

We sell these in small waxed paper bags, and they are more filling than they look. A firm favourite with children, plus they are quite nutritious too. We have used Vanilla *(see page 36)* as a filling, but they work equally well with some of the more adventurous flavours such as Rhubarb and Strawberry Sorbet *(see page 82)*.

Makes about 30

185 g (6½ oz/1½ cups) plain (all-purpose) flour

80 g (3 oz/⅓ cup) granulated (raw) sugar

150 g (5 oz/⅔ cup) light brown sugar

1 teaspoon baking powder

½ teaspoon ground cinnamon

½ teaspoon salt

300 g (10½ oz) jumbo oats, preferably organic

160 g (5½ oz) raisins

250 ml (8½ fl oz) vegetable or sunflower oil

90 ml (3½ fl oz) whole milk

3 medium eggs

Preheat the oven to 170°C (340°F/Gas 3°). Line 3 baking sheets with baking parchment paper, or use silicone mats.

Mix together the flour, both the sugars, baking powder, cinnamon and salt in a food processor. Next add the oats and raisins followed by the oil, milk, and eggs. Mix well. The mixture will be quite runny so don't be alarmed.

Drop 1 heaped tablespoon of the mixture on to the prepared baking sheet for each biscuit. These are large biscuits, so about 6 should fit on a sheet.

Again, spread each spoonful of mixture with your hands or a spoon into a 6 cm (2½ in) wide circle. Leave space in between each one as they can spread when cooking

Bake one biscuit first for 10–12 minutes or until golden brown. If the timing and temperature is coorect bake the rest of the biscuits accordingly.

Let the biscuits completely cool on a wire rack before sandwiching with ice cream. Wrap the 'sandwiches' in waxed or greaseproof paper and keep in the freezer until ready to serve.

I find these biscuits a little heavy and squishy to eat on their own, but they are absolutely perfect for freezing with ice cream or sorbet.

BRANDY PARFAIT

We use this in a ball in the centre of our Christmas bombes *(see page 50)*. Remember that it will never freeze really hard due to the alcohol content.

125 g (4 oz/½ cup) caster (superfine) sugar

120 ml (4 fl oz) egg yolks (approximately 4–5 medium eggs)

300 ml (10 fl oz) double cream

90 ml (3 fl oz) brandy

Put the sugar in a saucepan with 130 ml (4½ fl oz) water and bring to the boil. Stir until the sugar dissolves and you have a sugar syrup. Set on one side to cool. The temperature should be around 30°C (86°F) when you whisk the syrup into the eggs.

Place the egg yolks in a bain-marie and whisk until light and creamy. Do not overwhisk, you don't really want any froth.

Place the bain-marie over a medium heat. Whisk the cooled syrup slowly into the egg yolks, so they don't scramble, until the temperature reaches 85°C (185°F) and the mixture has thickened.

Bear in mind that this is a slow process and can take up to 20 minutes. The volume of the mixture should have increase by about 50 per cent.

Remove from the heat and put in a large mixing bowl. Then with an electric whisk on medium speed, whisk for around 10 minutes. Once the volume has increased by a further 50 per cent and the mixture is thick enough to hold a ribbon trail, place it in the fridge.

Pour the cream into a medium-sized bowl and whip until it forms soft peaks. Leave to chill for 2 hours.

Remove egg and syrup mixture from the fridge, carefully fold in the whipped cream alternating with the tablespoons of brandy, trickled down the inside of the bowl. Pour the mixture into the ice-cream maker and churn.

Spoon the churned parfait into a container. Place it in the freezer until ready to serve.

ICE CREAM BOMBE

A party favourite, ice cream bombes are stunning in both appearance and taste. We use professional silicone moulds from Italy, but you can buy aluminium hemisphere cake pans and line them with clingfilm. You can also buy demisphere moulds in sheets from good kitchen suppliers. To make the ice cream bombe, use the same moulds as you would for the Ice Cream Balls (see page 110), depending on the number of layers that you want and the sizes of the mould you can obtain.

These bombes are simpler to build compared to the balls as you don't need to align each half. You always start with the smaller centre and work outwards. As with the balls, sorbets work better as an inside layer rather than the final outer layer as they tend to melt quickly.

Place the sheet of small demispheres on a freezerproof board and fill one with the required flavour of ice cream or sorbet (churned so that it is not completely solid and can be poured into the mould).

You only need fill one mould for the centre of your bombe. Smooth the surface with a spatula, so that it is completely flat. Place in the freezer and leave until completely frozen.

Line 2 freezerproof boards with waxed paper. Remove your ice cream or sorbet from the mould and place on one of the prepared boards.

For the outside, if you cannot get hold of silicone moulds, use aluminium ones lined with clingfilm – this will make it easy to turn the ice cream out. With silicone moulds you can just flip the ice cream out.

Almost fill the next size mould then drop in the small frozen centre, smoothing the surface with a spatula. Place in the freezer and leave until completely frozen. Remove from the mould and place on the remaining prepared board.

Keep doing this with your moulds going up in size each time. Our bombes usually consist of 3 layers. It is important to smooth the surface each time, so that you end up with a bombe that sits neatly on your plate.

Unmould the largest one and sit it on a cake board. Keep in the freezer until required.

You can decorate the top with berries or currants. I usually put half a cocktail stick down the centre to hold the decoration. Redcurrants work really well.

ICE CREAM BALLS

Sorbets are suitable for the inside of these ice cream balls, but not on the outside as they melt more quickly. Flavours that work well together are Raspberry Sorbet (see page 56) with Rice Pudding (see page 47) or Christmas Ice Cream (see page 50) with Brandy Parfait centre (see page 107).

To make an ice cream ball firstly you need to create the centre. Place a sheet of small demispheres on a freezerproof board and fill with the required flavour of ice cream or sorbet (churned so that it is not completely solid and can be poured into the moulds). You will need to fill 2 to make one ball. Smooth the surface with a spatula, so that it is completely flat. Place in the freezer.

Once these are completely frozen, heat the spatula with some boiling water then thoroughly dry it. If you leave the spatula wet then there will be ice between the layer. Slightly melt the surface of the demispheres and unmould one half and join together to form a sphere. Try not to handle them too much as they will melt.

Put a sheet of baking parchment or greaseproof paper on a freezerproof board and place the sphere on top. Return to the freezer.

For the outside, if you cannot get hold of silicone moulds use aluminium ones lined with clingfilm – the clingfilm will make it easy to turn the ice cream out. With silicone moulds you can just flip the ice cream out. You will need 2 moulds per layer.

Place one of the moulds on a freezerproof board. Do exactly the same as before with a thickly churned mix and almost fill the mould then drop in the small frozen centre. Ours is off centre, but you can do as you wish. Approximately half of it should be sticking out of the top.

When this has completelty frozen, churn some more of your mix and almost fill the second mould. Remove the mould from the frozen section then, being carful to align the two halves, place the frozen half with the small sphere sticking out on top of the second mould, creating a sphere. Return to the freezer.

Once completely frozen unmould. You may need to slice a tiny portion of the bottom to prevent your creation from rolling away. Place in the freezer until ready to serve.

PISTACHIO, ROSEWATER AND CARDAMOM ICE CREAM KULFI

This is a hint of Indian Kulfi on a stick. A perfect dessert for a spicy curry – cooling and fragrant on the tongue.

---

800 ml (27 fl oz)
Basic Sweetened Ice
Cream Mix (see page 14)

1½ tablespoons
pistachio paste
(see suppliers page 152)

2 tablespoons
rosewater
(I use Mymoune brand
– see suppliers page 152)

½ teaspoon
cardamom extract

75 g (2½ oz)
unsalted pistachios,
finely chopped

Make the basic sweetened mix to the point where you have stirred it for 4 minutes or so.

Remove from the heat, add the pistachio paste to the hot mix and whisk together until well incorporated.

Add the rosewater and cardamom extract and cool down to 4°C (39°F) within 90 minutes. You can cool down the mixture more quickly by placing it in a pan in a sink with cold water and ice cubes, or putting the mix in a Ziploc bag inside a pan of cold water with ice cubes.

Once the mixture has cooled, keep it in the fridge. Add the pistachios, place the mix in the ice cream maker and churn.

Put the churned mix into Kulfi moulds or something of a similar shape. When partially frozen, insert the sticks. Once completely frozen, wrap a cool, damp cloth around the mould and pull the kulfi out.

Roll in the chopped pistachio and place back in the freezer on a board until ready to serve.

Delicate decoratives

Presentation is always important and there are many decorative additions that will enhance your creations: an Ice Bowl (see page 124), for example, can look spectacular and make an impressive centre piece. I like to think of decoration as actively complementing your work through taste, colour or texture.

Meringues (see page 118) not only use your surplus egg whites, but they also add a delightful crunch to a Raspberry Ripple (see page 137); Candied Citrus Peel (see page 128) adds a sharp yet sweet textural chewiness which adds another dimension, as well as maximising your use of the fruit; home-baked Wafers (see page 146) are crisp, crunchy and buttery; while Chocolate Teaspoons (see page 148) add an element of humour and, of course, the pleasure of chocolate.

Delicate decoratives

MERINGUES

You can make wafers and meringues with the egg whites that you will have left over from the ice cream recipes. Obviously you may make more than this, as long as you follow the same ratio of one part egg white to one and a half parts caster (superfine) sugar.

Makes 10 large meringues or 20 small ones

80 ml (2½ fl oz) egg whites (2–3)

120 g (scant 4 oz/½ cup) caster (superfine) sugar

Preheat the oven to 140°C (275°F/Gas ½).

Place the egg whites in a food processor or use an electric whisk and whisk until stiff. When you turn the bowl upside down the egg whites should not fall out.

On a slow speed, whisk in half the sugar. Once it's incorporated, carefully fold in the rest of the sugar with a metal spoon.

Line a baking tray, preferably with a silicone mat or baking parchment, although waxed paper can be difficult to peel off the meringue, once it is cold.

Depending on whether you want small or large meringues, spoon the mixture on to the tray with either a tablespoon or teaspoon.

Bake in the preheated oven: the smaller meringues should take about 40 minutes; the larger ones about 70 minutes, but bear in mind that domestic ovens do vary, so keep an eye on them.

I usually bake meringues at night and don't open the oven door or remove them from the oven until they are completely cold the next morning. They should then be slightly chewy in the centre.

CRYSTALLISED ROSE PETALS

These make a stunning decorative addition to your ice cream and are easy to make, once you know how. I made the mistake of immersing the whole petal in egg white when I first tried to make these, and ended up with a heavy, soggy mess. The trick is to be deft and delicate with a light touch. They make great decorations for Valentine's day, weddings and birthdays. They truly are a way to impress all your friends and family.

1 egg white

1 tablespoon caster (superfine) sugar

1 rose head, freshly picked

Break the egg in a bowl and separate it. You will only need the whites. Whisk until light and frothy.

With a small, clean paintbrush, lightly coat each rose petal with the frothy part of the egg white, then sprinkle the sugar over and voila! You have sugared rose petals – very beautiful.

HOLLY LEAVES CUT OUT

These make great decorations for Ice Cream Balls *(see page110)*. I like to use them to decorate my Christmas cake and ball *(see page 50)*. For the cut-out ice cream shapes use a plain ice cream such as Chocolate or Vanilla *(see pages 28 and 36)*. Anything with a ripple will melt too quickly.

Once you have churned your ice cream, take a baking tray 20 x 30 x 5 cm (8 x 12 x 2 in), line it with a silicone mat and spread an layer of ice cream over, approximately 1.5 cm (¾ in) deep.

Freeze for 1–2 hours then, using pastry cutters, cut out the shapes required. Place these on on a silicone mat and return to the freezer until ready to use.

You can experiment with all sorts of cutter shapes, from hearts to flowers – have fun with them, and add that elegant touch to your chosen dessert.

ICE BOWLS

Ice bowls and plates are a very pretty way to serve your ice creams or sorbets. As well as oranges and other citrus fruit, you could use slices of strawberry, redcurrants, bay leaves, mint and star anise – you are only limited by your imagination.

You will need two stainless-steel bowls; one should fit inside the other with approximately 2 cm (¾ in) between them. Line the smaller bowl with a piece of clingfilm, fill it until ¾ full with water and freeze (this is going to weigh it down and prevent it moving).

Once the small bowl has frozen, remove from the freezer. Place the larger bowl on a freezerproof board, then place the smaller bowl inside.

Slice some oranges, or whatever you fancy, quite thinly and pierce one edge of each slice with a cocktail stick. Wedge the orange slices between the 2 bowls with the cocktail stick resting over the top. This prevents the slices sinking to the bottom of your ice bowl.

Now pour water into the larger bowl to 1 cm (½ in) from the top – do not fill it right up as water expands as it freezes.

Freeze overnight, then remove. Let stand at room temperature then use a hot cloth carefully remove the smaller bowl and its ice, this could take 20 minutes or so, don't force it or the ice bowl will crack.

Once the smaller bowl has come away invert the larger bowl and free the ice bowl again using a hot cloth. Carefully remove the cocktail sticks or snip off with a pair of scissors. Freeze until needed.

Variations

Ice plates

For this you need a small, round silicone mould. Place the mould on a freezerproof board. Pour water in up to 1 cm (½ in) from the top. Don't fill it all the way up as water expands as it freezes.

Across the base spread lemon or lime slices, blueberries, vine leaves, whatever you fancy, as long as it is fairly flat, or slices of strawberry rather than whole strawberries. The fruit will float around if you're not careful, so take it out of the freezer after 45 minutes or so and check. Manoeuvre the decorations into place if you need to.

Once frozen, flip the plate out of the silicone mould and use as a serving plate. Small ones are very impressive to serve individual desserts on.

FLOWER MOULDS

I find that sorbet gives a more defined shape to intricate moulds than ice cream, so I tend to use the chrysanthemum moulds, with more detail for sorbets and the softer rose moulds for ice cream.

There is a whole array of different silicone moulds on the market, with some suppliers listed at the back of this book *(see page 152)*. It is very easy to produce some lovely flowers and wacky shapes. You don't need to churn the mix, but you must try and eliminate air bubbles.

To make your flowers, place the moulds of roses or chrysanthemums (or whatever shape you have chosen), on a freezerproof board.

Pour your ice cream or sorbet into the moulds and gently bang the bottom of the board to release any air bubbles that may have settled at the bottom. You can also use a sterilised knitting needle to swirl around the mix to try and release them. I find that the smaller the mould the more air bubbles. Don't completely fill the moulds because the contents will expand once frozen.

Place on a level shelf in the coldest part of the freezer, usually the bottom, overnight then unmould. The colder the moulds, the easier it is to peel them off.

Keep them in the freezer until ready to serve.

CANDIED CITRUS PEEL

This is a great way to use up the skins of expensive fruits, such as Amalfi lemons. The candied peel is lovely to decorate and scatter through ice creams and sorbets. It is also very pretty on top of cakes.

Makes approximately 30 peels, depending on the size of the fruit

2 oranges, limes or lemons

300 g (10½ oz/1¾ cups) caster (superfine) or granulated (raw) sugar

Cut the fruit in half and juice them. Put the juice to one side.

Cut each fruit half in half again and scrape out the pulp with a spoon. Scrape off some of the pith, but don't remove it all as I think it adds to the flavour. Cut the peel into thin slices about 0.5 cm (¼ in) each.

Place the peel in a saucepan and cover with cold water. Bring to the boil over high heat, then remove from the heat and drain the water away. Repeat this for a total of three times and set the peel aside.

Mix the sugar in the pan with 135 ml (4½ fl oz) water and stir over a high heat until the sugar has dissolved. Use a sugar thermometer and heat until the temperature reaches 110°C (230°F).

Lower the heat and add the citrus peel. You can remove the thermometer at this stage. Simmer for 30–90 minutes until the peel is all translucent.

Remove the peel from the syrup with a slotted spoon and place individually and spread out (not as a great heap), on a rack over a tray to dry.

Depending on the humidity peel can dry in a few hours or a few days, or you can put them in an oven on a very low temperature to hurry this up.

They can be partially dipped in chocolate or rolled in caster sugar

Keep the syrup in a jar and use it as a substitute for sugar syrup when making sorbets: it is very sweet and tastes of the fruit.

Toppings

Tufnell Park Honey

150g

M J Balston
14 Mercers Road
London N19 4PJ
Produce of UK
BBE 2013

This chapter is made up of a selection of ripples, sauces and extras that you can mix into your ice cream or serve as an accompaniment for added flavour and appeal.

I use ripples to swirl into and on top of ice creams and find it works better if the ripple is carefully folded rather than stirred into the ice cream. This way it remains distinct and does not blend with the ice cream.

My sauces are served as an accompaniment, either poured over the ice cream or served in a jug on the side. The sauces are not suitable for freezing. In winter the thought of chocolate or caramel sauce heated and poured over a simple bowl of vanilla ice cream is enough to warm even the coldest of hearts.

The extras are scattered on top of ice creams or in small pieces within the ice cream. Make sure the sizes are manageable as these some of these extras are brittles and can catch you unaware when frozen.

Toppings

BLACKCURRANT RIPPLE

Blacurrant has an intense flavour. Combine with liquorice to make a beautiful Liquorice and Blackcurrant Ice Cream (see page 42). This is a personal favourite combination of mine as it reminds me of those delicious old-fashioned sweets!

Makes 500 ml (17 fl oz)

400 g (14 oz)
frozen blackcurrants

200 g (7 oz/scant 1 cup)
granulated (raw) sugar

25 ml (1 fl oz)
lemon juice

Place the fruit, sugar and 150 ml (5 fl oz) water into a large pan and bring to the boil, stirring regularly. Reduce the heat until the mixture is simmering, then continue to simmer for 8–10 minutes, or until the fruit has broken down. I like quite a tart flavour, but add more sugar to taste if you wish.

Strain the fruit mixture through a fine sieve into a clean pan, squeezing any additional juice out of the fruit by pressing it down with the back of a spoon.

Return the strained fruit juice to the heat and bring it to a simmer. Continue to simmer for about 20 minutes until the mixture is syrupy and thick like a jam.

Set aside until completely cooled. Keep in the fridge for up to 1 week.

LEMON SAUCE

Thank you to David Lebovitz for this recipe and for being such an ice cream inspiration.

Makes 250 ml (8½ fl oz)

200 g (7 oz/scant 1 cup)
caster (superfine) sugar

60 ml (2 fl oz)
lemon juice
(approximately 2–3 lemons)

Scatter the sugar evenly across the bottom of a large saucepan. Pour 125 ml (4 fl oz) water and 1 tablespoon of the lemon juice over the top of the sugar over a medium heat until the sugar begins to dissolve, but don't stir.

When the sugar starts smoking and turning brown take the pan off the heat and carefully add a further 125 ml (4 fl oz) water, whisking until smooth (it will be very hot, so take care).

Stir in 2 tablespoons of the lemon juice and allow to cool to room temperature.

Once cool, strain through a sieve to remove any undissolved sugar.

Once the lemony sauce reaches room temperature taste and add a further 1 tablespoon lemon juice if you wish.

This sauce can be served at any temperature and will keep in the fridge for 4–5 weeks.

RASPBERRY RIPPLE

Churn with Vanilla *(see page 36)* for the classic raspberry ripple ice cream.

Makes 150 ml (5 fl oz)

400 g (14 oz)
fresh or frozen raspberries

80 g (3oz/ ⅓ cup)
granulated (raw) sugar

Heat the fruit, sugar and 45 ml (2 fl oz) water (only add the water if using fresh raspberries) into a large saucepan and bring the mixture to the boil, stirring regularly. Reduce the heat until the mixture is simmering, then continue to simmer for 8–10 minutes, or until the fruit has broken down.

Strain the fruit mixture through a sieve into a clean pan, squeezing any additional juice out of the fruit by pressing it down with the back of a spoon.

Return the strained fruit juice to the heat and bring it to a simmer. Continue to simmer until the mixture is syrupy and thick like a jam.

Set aside until completely cooled. Store in the fridge for up to 1 week.

RASPBERRY SAUCE

Delicious drizzled over Chocolate Ice Cream *(see page 28)*.

Makes 200 ml (6¾ fl oz)

400 g (14 oz)
fresh or frozen raspberries

3–4 tablespoons
caster (superfine) sugar

2 tablespoons
lemon juice
(approximately
1 lemon)

60 ml (2 fl oz)
sugar syrup
(see page 17)

Puree the raspberries with 3 tablespoons (50 g/2 oz) of the sugar and the sugar syrup in a food processor until you have a smooth puree.

Press the puree through a sieve into a bowl and stir in the lemon juice to taste.

Taste and add any remaining sugar if preferred.

Serve chilled or at room temperature. This sauce will keep for up to 1 week in the fridge.

STRAWBERRY RIPPLE

This is delicious rippled through Peanut Butter and Chocolate Ice Cream *(see pages 44 and 28)*.

Makes 200 ml (6¾ fl oz)

250 g (9 oz)
fresh strawberries,
hulled

40 g (1½ oz)
vanilla sugar

2 teaspoons
lemon juice

1 vanilla pod,
split lengthwise and
seeds scraped out
(use the pod and seeds)

Place a saucer in the freezer.

Put the strawberries, sugar, lemon juice and vanilla pod into a thick bottomed pan and bring to the boil. Boil for about 15 minutes, stirring regularly and checking the setting point every minute or so during the last 5 minutes.

To do this, take the cold saucer out of the freezer, put a little jam on it, and put it back in to cool for a minute. If it wrinkles when you push it with your finger, then it's done. It should be syrupy and thick like a jam. Skim any scum from the surface of the jam.

Remove the vanilla pod and set aside until completely cooled. Store in the fridge for up to 1 week.

SEVILLE ORANGE MARMALADE RIPPLE

Seville oranges are bitter oranges, grown throughout the Mediterranean. They are highly aromatic, with a noticeably thick and dimpled skin but are not suitable for eating on their own. They are in season for a very short time in the UK from the end of December to February. Make the most of them by making your own marmalade. This lovely, tangy ripple works well with Chocolate Ice Cream as well as Vanilla *(see pages 28 and 36)*.

Makes around five 454 g (1 lb) jars

700 g (1lb 9oz) Seville oranges

90 ml (3½ fl oz) lemon juice (approximately 2 lemons)

1.4 kg (3lb/6 cups) granulated (raw) sugar

Place a saucer in the freezer.

Put the oranges in a large pan with 1.2 litres (2 pints) water, bring to the boil and simmer for about 2 hours.

Allow to cool so that the oranges are easy to handle, then remove the oranges leaving the water in the pan.

Cut up the oranges, including the pulp, into peel (the thickness will depend on your personal preference).

Remove the pips and transfer to a small pan with a small amount of water to cover. Boil for 5 minutes, then strain the pips out.

Put the chopped oranges, strained liquid and lemon juice in the pan of cooking water. Add the sugar and stir over a low heat until dissolved. Bring to the boil and cook until set.

Test for setting by placing a teaspoon of marmalade on the chilled saucer. Return it to the freezer for a minute, then push the marmalade with your finger. If a skin forms, the marmalade is set. If not, continue cooking for a few more minutes and keep testing.

Take off the heat then remove any scum with a slotted spoon. Stir to ensure even distribution of peel and pot into warmed clean jam jars. Leave to cool before the lids are fixed.

Variations

Chilli marmalade

Add 1 small chilli chopped, to every litre of marmalade.

Ginger marmalade

Add a piece of fresh root ginger, 2.5 x 5cm (1 x 2 in), peeled and roughly chopped into four pieces, plus 1 teaspoon of stem ginger, chopped, to every 750 ml (25 fl oz) marmalade.

CHOCOLATE SAUCE

A classic sauce that goes with absolutely any flavoured ice cream. This makes a great ripple accompaniment to Orange and Candied Peel (see page 40) and White Chocolate and Toasted Coconut Ice Cream (see page 27).

Makes 150 ml (5 fl oz)

100 g (3½ oz)
plain chocolate
(at least 60% cocoa solids)
either as callets
or finely chopped

100 ml (3½ fl oz)
double cream

Melt the chocolate in a bain-marie, then whisk in the double cream.

This sauce should be served hot. It will keep for a week in the fridge, but may need a little more cream or hot water to thin it down.

MOCHA RIPPLE

Ripple through through Tiramasu Ice Cream (see page 34) for a rich coffee flavour.

**Makes 200 ml
(6 ¾ fl oz)**

80 g (3 oz)
granulated (raw) sugar

40 ml (1½ fl oz)
agave syrup

125 ml (4 fl oz)
espresso or strong
instant coffee

50 g (2 oz)
cocoa powder

Whisk all the ingredients together in a pan over a medium heat until it starts to bubble, then simmer for 3–4 minutes.

Allow the mixture to cool. When it is cold it will be thick and viscous, perfect for rippling through or on top of ice cream.

Keep in an airtight container in the fridge for up to two weeks.

FLEUR DE SEL CARAMEL SAUCE

French *Fleur de sel* is important as it imparts a very particular flavour and intensity, which I have not been able to replicate with other salt.

Makes 3 small jars

225g (8 oz/1 cup) granulated (raw) sugar

2 tablespoons agave Nectar

250ml (8½ fl oz) double cream

1½ teaspoon *Fleur de sel* salt

150 ml (5 fl oz) soured cream (made with 100ml (3 ½ fl oz) double cream and 50 ml (2 fl oz) lemon juice)

Put the sugar, agave and 150 ml (5 fl oz) water together in a medium-sized saucepan with the sugar thermometer. Bring to the boil over a high heat until the sugar has dissolved.

Meanwhile, heat the cream and salt in another saucepan until the salt has dissolved and the cream has come to a boil. Remove and set aside.

Continue to heat the sugar mix until it reaches 180°C (350°F). It should be quite dark, just on the verge of being burnt. Remove from the heat and let it sit for a moment.

Whisk the hot cream and salt into the hot sugar mix. It will spit as you do this, so be careful this doesn't bubble up over the edge of the pan. As it is extremely hot, it may be better to place the pan in the bottom of a stainless-steel sink.

Whisk in the soured cream and leave to cool. Once cooled, store in an air-tight container and keep refridgerated until required.

Ripple through Salted Caramel Ice Cream *(see page 48)* or any ice cream flavour of your choice.

ALMOND NUT BRITTLE

We layer this through the Salted Caramel Ice Cream (see page 48), but it can adorn any ice cream or be eaten on its own. We use it to decorate the tops of our Ice Cream Cake (see page 94)

---

100 g (3½ oz)
almonds with skins on

150 g (5 oz/scant ¾ cup)
granulated (raw) sugar

Toast the almonds on a baking tray at 180°C (350°F/Gas 4) for 10–15 minutes.

Leave in the oven to keep warm.

Melt 50 g (2 oz) of the sugar in a pan, on a medium heat. When melted, add another 50 g (2 oz), allow this to melt then add the remaining 50 g (2 oz) and allow it to melt.

When the sugar is a nice, liquid dark brown, add the warm toasted almonds and stir until they are all covered with the caramel. Pour on to a baking tray making one even layer and leave to cool. When cool, chop into small pieces. Alternatively, put in a food processor and finely chop.

Store in an airtight container, otherwise it goes sticky and keep for up to one month.

TOFFEE CHUNKS

Combine with the ice cream of your choice for that delicious sticky toffee flavour.

---

475 g (1 lb/2 cups)
caster (superfine) sugar

250 g (9 oz/1 cup)
butter

60 ml (2 fl oz)
golden syrup

Combine all the ingredients in a large saucepan with 60 ml (2 fl oz) water and bring to the boil, stirring until everything is well mixed and the sugar has dissolved.

Stop stirring and continue to boil until the temperature reaches 140°C (275°F/Gas ½) and the mixture is dark golden in colour.

Pour into a small, metal tray approximately 20 x 30 cm (8 x 12 in) and leave until set. Do not pour on to waxed paper and leave, as it's impossible to remove the wax paper.

Cut into 1 cm squares and scatter through ice cream once churned. It's perfect with Chocolate Ice Cream (see page 28) or Vanilla Ice Cream (see page 36).

WAFERS

Wafers are a great accompaniment to any flavoured ice cream. We love to serve our wafers with the Ice Cream Blocks *(see page 100)*, to make a delicious ice cream-type sandwich!

150 g (5 oz/1¼ cups) icing (confectioners') sugar

175 g (6 oz/1½ cups) plain (all-purpose) flour

1 teaspoon cornflour

175 ml (6 fl oz) egg white (approximately 6 egg whites)

about 100 g (3½ oz) butter, melted

Preheat the oven to 170°C (340°F/Gas 3).

Sieve together the icing sugar, plain flour and cornflour into the food processor, add the egg whites and blend. Once blended together, dribble the melted butter down the inside of the bowl, then process again.

The mixture should be the consistency of a thick honey, as it needs to be spread evenly and thinly. If it is too thick, add a little extra melted butter.

Put 150 g (5 oz) of the mixture on to a baking tray covered with a silicone mat approximately 30 x 30 cm (12 x 12 in) and spread very thinly with the back of a palette knife, until it is the thickness of paper.

Bake in the preheated oven for 5 minutes. Remove from the oven and turn up the heat to 190°C (375°F/Gas 5).

Cut the mixture with biscuit cutters to the shapes required and place on a baking rack, so that the air can fully circulate, then return to the oven and bake for a further 5 minutes. Remove from the oven and leave to cool. Keep in an airtight box once cold.

AFFOGATO

Affogato means 'drowned' in Italian. It is a traditional Italian coffee-based dessert that consists of ice cream topped with a hot shot of fresh espresso. We used Salted Caramel Ice Cream *(see page 48)* to make ours.

To make your Affogato, scoop one large dollop of ice cream into a cup.

Make or buy an espresso, then drown your ice cream – the perfect morning wake up or an after dinner treat.

You can also top with Ameretto, or another similar tasting liqueur for a real flavour kick. Serve with Chocolate Spoons *(below)* for added bite.

CHOCOLATE TEASPOONS

You can try all sorts of flavours for this particular edible decoration, but I prefer using chocolate. Feel free to experiment with mould shapes and sizes – I particularly love these spoon-shaped moulds, and they are a firm favourite with our customers too!

50 g (2 oz) plain chocolate (at least 60% cocoa solids) either as callets or grated

Melt the chocolate in a bain-marie and pour into your spoon moulds.

With a spatula make sure the surface is absolutely even.

Leave to cool and, when completely solid, unmould.

Serve with the ice cream of your choice. We love serving our spoons with Affogato *(above)* or a strong cup of good quality coffee – delicious!

CHOCOLATE AND HAZELNUT TOFFEE CRUNCH

This is delicious with Vanilla *(see page 36)* or Chocolate *Ice Cream (see page 28)* or simply eat on its own.

225 g (8 oz/scant 2 cups) toasted skinless hazelnuts, chopped coarsely

1 teaspoon vanilla extract

¼ teaspoon baking powder

115 g (3¾ oz) butter

pinch of salt

200 g (7 oz/scant 1 cup) granulated sugar

50 g (2 oz) light brown muscovado sugar

140 g (4½ oz) dark chocolate callets

a sprinking of Fleur de sel salt, to garnish

Sprinkle the hazelnuts on to a silicone mat on a baking tray in a square about 20 x 20 cm (8 x 8 in) and toast the hazelnuts at 180°C (350°F/Gas 4) for 10–15 minutes. Leave in the oven to keep warm.

Measure out the vanilla extract and baking powder and have it ready.

Put a thermometer in a saucepan then heat the butter, salt, brown and white sugar and 2 tablespoons water, stirring occasionally, until it reaches 150°C (300°F).

Place the saucepan in the sink if you have a stainless-steel sink and use a long-handled wooden spoon to stir in the baking soda and vanilla extract. Be careful as this is very hot and is apt to spill out of the saucepan.

Remove the tray of nuts from the oven and swiftly pour the mixture evenly over the nuts on to the tray.

Scatter the chocolate callets over the top followed by a sprinkling of Fleur de sel.

Leave for 20 minutes or so until cool and break into small chunks. Store in an airtight container for up to one month.

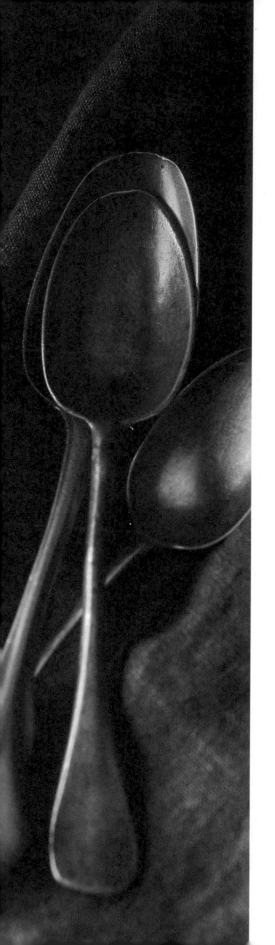

Suppliers

INGREDIENTS:

Pistachio paste, hazelnut paste, speciality nuts
Whynut
www.whynutshop.co.uk

Vanilla pods and extract
Vanilla Bazaar
www.vanillabazaar.com

Amarelli spezzata liquorice pellets
www.allthingsliquorice.co.uk

Cardamom extract from Spices of India
www.spicesofindia.co.uk

Mymoune rosewater
www.mymoune.com

Green Tea Fuji Matcha
The Japan Centre
www.japancentre.com
www.mountfuji.co.uk

Black sesame seeds
Chinese supermarket, or online
www.healthysupplies.co.uk

Hot chilli sauce
The Rib Man
www.theribman.co.uk

Callebaut chocolate callets
www.hbingredients.co.uk

Agave nectar
Groovy foods
www.groovyfood.co.uk

Cropwell Bishop Stilton cheese
www.cropwellbishopstilton.com

Niepoort white port
www.niepoort-vinhos.com/en/

Belvoir organic elderflower cordial
www.belvoirfruitfarms.co.uk

Glucose/dextrose powder
The Japan Centre
www.hollandbarrett.com

Fleur de sel salt
some branches of Marks and Spencers
www.ocado.com

EQUIPMENT:

Cuisinart for ice-cream machines
www.cuisinart.co.uk

Zeroll ice cream scoop
www.zeroll.com

Silikomart moulds
www.abbiamo.co.uk
www.silikomart.com

Other moulds
Lakeland
www.lakeland.co.uk
eBay

Zaksenberg Juicer
www.zaksenberg.com

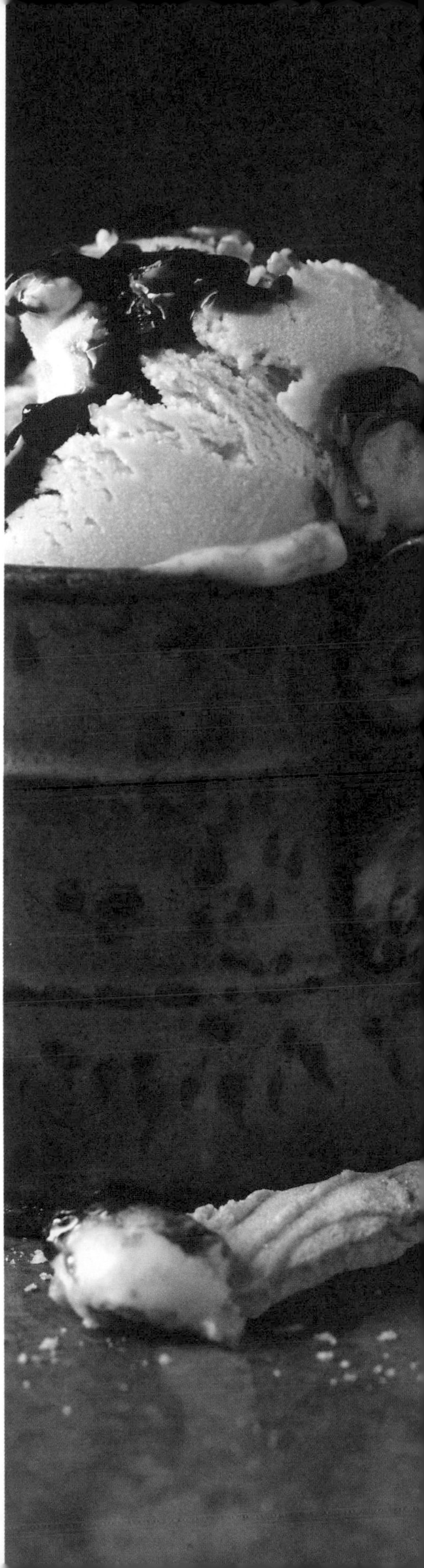

Acknowledgements

I WOULD LIKE TO PAY
PARTICULAR THANKS TO:

Gianina Popescu
Francesca Dale
Laura Lawrence
Tufnell Park Honey
Deborah Schneebeli Morrell
Maurizio Florio
Danielle Wood
Debs Miller
Nancy Layton Cooke
Robert and Kathy Graham Harrison
Juliette Otterburn-Hall
Liz, Michal, Jonathon, Benedict and Phoebe Case
Jo, Bob, Isi, Livi, Olivia, Charlie Klaber
Sue Odell
Robert Brighouse
Duncan Watson-Steward at The Star pub
Martin Larnach at The Tufnell Park Tavern
Julie Friend at Flavours
Alison Wade
Karen Fitzsimon
Oonagh Hodges
Helen Shipsey
Manon and Gully
Stefanie Wooding
Edina Maguire
Eunice Goes
Alice Dwyer
Sebastien Webster
Toby Allen at Brockley Market

I WOULD ALSO LIKE TO THANK
MY LOVELY NEIGHBOURS FOR
TESTING EVERYTHING!

References

Caroline and Robin Weir *Ice Creams, Sorbets and Gelati*

David Lebowitz *The Perfect Scoop*

Elizabeth David Harvest, *The Cold Months*

Mrs Marshall *The Book of Ices 1885*

Niki Segnit *The Flavour Thesaurus*

Index

Page numbers in *italics* refer to illustrations

Ruby Violet's Ice Cream Dreams 2013 by Julie Fisher

First published in 2013 by Hardie Grant Books

Hardie Grant Books (UK)
Dudley House, North Suite
34–35 Southampton Street
London WC2E 7HF

www.hardiegrant.co.uk

Hardie Grant Books (Australia)
Ground Floor, Building 1
658 Church Street
Melbourne, VIC 3121

www.hardiegrant.com.au

British Library Cataloguing-in-Publication Data. A catalogue record for this book is available from the British Library.

ISBN 978-1-74270-593-4

Commissioning Editor: Kate Pollard

Desk Editor: Kajal Mistry

Cover and Internal design: Jo and Graeme Garden

Photography and retouching: Danielle Wood

Food styling by Debbie Miller

Cover retouching by Butterfly Creative Services

Colour reproduction by p2D

Printed and bound China by 1010 Printing International Limited

10 9 8 7 6 5 4 3 2